Rewriting the Past

Rewriting the Past

2019 GLVWG Anthology

Greater Lehigh Valley Writers Group
Members

Greater Lehigh Valley Publishing Group

Rewriting the Past
2019 GLVWG Anthology

©2019 Greater Lehigh Valley Publishing Group (glvwg.org)

ISBN-13: 978-1-7336786-0-5

Acknowledgments

Anthology Chair
Donna Brennan
DegunkingLife.com

Content & Developmental Editing
Donna Brennan, Kelly Craig Decker, John Evans,
Phil Giunta, D.T. Krippene,
Christopher D. Ochs, Bernadette Sukley

Line & Copy Editing Staff
Pattie Giordani, Brenda Havens, Dianna Sinovic

Book Design & Format
Christopher D. Ochs
anigrafx.com

Cover art photograph by Mysticsartdesign
used by permission from pixabay.com

Other Anthologies by
the Greater Lehigh Valley Writers Group

GLVWG Writes Stuff
2015

Write Here, Write Now
2016

The Write Connections
2017

Table of Contents

Introduction
Donna Brennan

The Greater Lehigh Valley Writers Group (GLVWG) is a local and dynamic group of published and unpublished authors. Currently, GLVWG has well over 100 active members. Since its inception over 20 years ago, GLVWG has supported the talents and ambitions of its members in a variety of ways including monthly meetings and presentations, author nights at local bookstores and other venues, library talks (providing an avenue for members to speak to the public), and our annual conference (The Write Stuff).

The GLVWG Anthology is another avenue to benefit our members, showcasing their talents, and helping new authors learn the ropes of submitting their work for publication and the process of working with editors.

In addition to providing a means to showcase their work, the GLVWG Anthology serves to teach our members valuable aspects of self-publishing. Hopefully, if they decide to self-publish their own work, they will find the task less daunting because of what they've learned of the process.

But the book you hold in your hands—*Rewriting the Past*—is more than just a collection of stories, poems, and essays. It is a mechanism that can transport you, the reader into the thoughts and hearts of the authors who put so much of themselves into their work. Stories of how they wish they could change the past, of how they've accepted the past, or of how they've changed their perspective of the past. Some stories based on fact; some completely comprised of fiction. Essays that make the reader think, poems that are moving and tender, works of fiction that can make you smile or shed a tear.

This is what writing is all about. It's making a connection with the reader, and giving them a glimpse in how you, the author, thinks.

I hope you enjoy reading these works by our members as much as we enjoyed writing them. And we'd appreciate your feedback on Amazon, GoodReads, our blog (glvwgwritestuffblog.wordpress.com) or Facebook (www.facebook.com/Greater-Lehigh-Valley-Writers-Group-GLVWG-165117371531)

✝

Essays

Despite My Yesterdays, I Live Today
Darlene A. McGarrity

I never realized my lifelong struggle with addiction was because I gripped my dark past with twisted memories of regret. There was so much about my story I wanted to change, in the hope that changing my past would change my inner essence. All my dark nights of solitude and fantasizing about being seven, ten, or fourteen again and just having forethought back in the 80's. How great my life would be right now if I could just go back and not be there at that one moment when that awful thing happened to me.

Decades of self-sabotage followed. Underage drinking, teen pregnancy, and dropping out of high school—not to mention getting married at sixteen —left a foul presence around my soul. I felt dirty and unworthy of anything good that came my way. I couldn't get in front of any of it and my hope waned. I felt cheated out of an important part of my youth.

But that poor girl who dropped out of high school and got married before her friends graduated didn't have to be me. That girl, sucked into the cycle of abuse with an older boy, didn't have to hold onto pain and the anguish of guilt. That girl, who once drank too much, could now face a clearer reality and use it to shape her future.

After years of meetings, quiet moments in parks and meditation, I had an idea. I would tell my story in a way that made me a victor instead of a victim.

My story didn't require a negative stain on my identity. My children could learn how the trials and errors of a volatile life of shame and regret helped me when I used them as a lesson instead of a curse.

I could remember my past in a way to help my coming years; maybe I did my best and it was always good enough. Maybe I was supposed to have my children young so my inexperience and youthful nature could be a backdrop for the powerful wisdom and knowledge I shared with them as they grew and ventured into life.

Instead of being a victim of older men with poor boundaries in an era when young girls had no voice, I changed my perception. I was no longer the "teenager who got knocked up at fifteen." I was the "girl who started her family early" so she could enjoy her time more as the kids got older. No more was I the "tramp who lost everything due to drugs and alcohol." Now, I was the young woman who figured out what didn't work and embraced what did to build a better life on the stepping stones of experience.

My retold story as a survivor instead of a victim would heal me later when I told it to strangers while we all clutched Styrofoam cups of strong coffee. They would tell me how brave I was to share such intimate self-awareness. They cried and confessed that my story helped them *heal*.

If they only knew how telling my rewritten story helped me more.

✝

Evolving Memories
Donna Brennan

Psychologists say memories are not perfect copies of what occurred; they are filtered by our minds as we store them, and are further modified and reconstructed with each recall.

This explains why you can have a memory so clear and vivid you are certain you remember exactly what happened, but someone else who was there remembers it very differently and is equally convinced that they remember it correctly.

For example, when I was in college, my roommate wanted to learn how to swim. Since I had taught swimming in high school, I drove her to the mall so she could buy a bathing suit and then we went to the campus pool. For years I believed I had let her down because we only made it to the pool three times.

We reconnected when we both worked in New York City. With a big smile she told my friend how she and I went to the campus pool "all the time." I didn't argue the point with her, but I was surprised we both had such different recall of how often we went swimming.

At the time I supposed she played the memory of those swim lessons in her mind again and again, and eventually all those recalls turned into additional trips we never made. But knowing what I now know about memory, I wonder if my own recall was colored by my guilt. Is it possible we did go more than three times?

More recently, a friend told me her first husband never spent time with their daughter when the child was an infant and toddler. One day the husband posed in a photo as if he were feeding their daughter in her highchair. He didn't really feed her—in fact, he never fed her. My friend kept this photo in a frame in her house.

By the time her daughter was four, my friend was divorced and remarried. The little girl saw her dad every other weekend. One day she told her mom that when she was younger her dad was the one who always fed her. I believe seeing that photo every day, multiple times most days, created a memory in her mind. That memory was consistent with what she wanted to believe and how much attention her dad gave her now.

Sometimes memories are more pleasant than the truth; sometimes they might be worse. A childhood friend of mine recalls being beat up by a sibling every day of her young life. I was at her house almost daily, and never saw or heard about it. None of her other siblings remember this ever happening—I think if it happened every day they'd remember at least one occurrence. It may have happened a few times, but I sincerely doubt it happened as often as she thinks it did.

Every time we remember something, we may be rewriting the past, just a little bit. Until it's a new story.

✝

The House That Got Away
Idelle Kursman

When my husband and I speak about the challenges of living in our house, I get into a reflective mood.

After two years of house-hunting, my husband and I narrowed it down to two—a reasonably priced starter house and a more expensive colonial on a cul-de-sac. The colonial was more spacious, particularly for its larger kitchen. I didn't like the bedrooms on the second floor because the walls had many strangely shaped angles. The house also needed a lot of work and was $20,000 more, which seemed like a fortune at the time. The smaller house boasted a big backyard on a quiet street. It was in move-in condition and looked very comfortable and inviting. Since the owner of the colonial refused to budge on the price, I thought we could start off in the smaller house and eventually move into a bigger one when we could afford it.

However, after we lived there for two years, I became frustrated with the small kitchen and the shortage of closet space. It has an eat-in kitchen, but there isn't enough counter space to comfortably prepare meals. Despite adding a clothing rack in the basement utility room and purchasing a makeshift closet, we still don't have enough room to hang up all our clothes. Through the years we considered buying another house, but there was always a problem. Either it was on a street with hills, the area was too congested, or there were serious flaws with the house itself. Housing prices also shot up substantially. So we never found another one to call home.

I occasionally feel down that we did not choose that colonial. Did we lose our chance to live a happier and more comfortable life or was moving into the house we have now meant to be and ultimately for the best? I often wish, if I could rewrite history, I would have chosen the house that got away.

But then I remember what we gained by living where we are now. My backyard is large and scenic, and we have had fun cookouts through the years. We did not have to make any changes for years after moving in, which was helpful because we were busy working and raising our twins. And talk about wonderful neighbors! I'll always remember my next-door neighbor driving me and my little sons to the emergency room when I had the most excruciating migraine headache. And my neighbor down the street—whom I enjoy taking walks with—we always confide, encourage, and support each other whenever one of us is having a problem.

So, although we've had to endure many frustrations, we've also enjoyed many benefits from the choice we made. Like everything in life, there are advantages and disadvantages. Besides, we plan to move in a year or two, so we still hope to buy our dream home then.

✝

Remembering Caroline
Rosanne Lamoreaux

Contrary to what the public may believe, the death of a patient is difficult on medical personnel. It saps them physically and mentally, and causes those involved to doubt their ability to heal. It makes them question every order followed, every medication given, and every treatment done.

As health providers, we're taught to stand tall in the face of a heartless adversary called "illness." We strive to be compassionate caregivers, relying on years of training and our continuing quest to learn more, arming ourselves with the latest technology and newest medications. Yet, occasionally there's a patient who affects the entire team, who creeps into their hearts and leaves a deep impression—the scar formed by their demise aching at unexpected moments, regardless of how much time has passed; the memory of their face or diagnosis or personality, as unforgettable as the events which occurred when the monitor alarms sounded.

When later asked, it's not uncommon for those on the team to be able to say who took the lead, who delivered compressions, who infused the IV medication, who intubated/connected the ventilator, and who drew the lab work or blood gases. Roles were automatically assumed, each person understanding without being told what had to be done. The code still vivid years later, with specific images deeply imbedded—staff persons recall the doctor preparing himself to speak with the family and the sobs that ensued; the nurse delicately washing the body, as the housekeeper picks up a mop to erase the controlled chaos that occurred; while the respiratory therapist discreetly removes the ventilator, and the unit aide goes for clean bed linen and a gown.

Rewriting the Past

Staff share the same sadness as they complete the tasks at hand with stoicism, though their emotions may be as varied as the colors on a spectrum. Afterwards, the death will be used as a teachable moment, in order to help improve the delivery of care in a highly technical and emotionally stressful environment.

I've cared for thousands of patients in 37 years, greeting each of them with a confident smile; understanding the importance of advocacy; patiently explaining until a person grasps their diagnosis, to help them make an educated decision, or to understand how to live with their disease. Sometimes it feels as if skills and clinical knowledge are not enough, when I realize that the chance to heal is gone, the patient will spend no more time with family or friends, or enjoying another day in the sun.

The past can't be rewritten. Although, at times I wish it could—especially those specific moments which arise in the middle of the night, as my mind rehashes past events and wishes I had pursued through lab work, vital signs and further testing, a gut feeling that something was wrong.

For medical personnel, the reality is: there are no second chances, no what-ifs, no going back in time and, definitely—no rewrites.

✝

Poems

Brave New World
Dawn M. Sooy

From England, they hoped to find
A new life, religious freedom, and land.
One ship broken, sadly left behind,
All crammed into one, very unplanned.

The treacherous journey, off course, unexplored,
With stormy high seas, freezing water, very cold.
Praying to their god, "Please, save us, oh Lord."
Days turned to weeks, their pleas tenfold.

At night they heard cannonballs booming.
Pirates were boarding and killing the crew.
Some gathering the pilgrims, others were looting.
The passengers' hopes for freedom fallen through.

The United States was never claimed
Until a Russian emperor, Peter the Great
Found this world, savage and untamed.
And now, dear reader, Добро пожаловать в царство*

* Welcome to Tsarland

✝

Frankly, My Dear
Paul Teese

Truth is overrated.
Give me a story instead,
a film, a blockbuster, beginning
with searchlights in a night sky,
or a roaring lion, or a silent snow-capped peak.
Tell me your tale, but shaped as a screenplay,
with tightened plot and sharpened dialogue.
Take up your blade, and leave the cutting room floor littered
with those failed and pointless outtakes,
the times you missed your mark,
forgot your lines.
Then assemble the rest,
and let your director's cut premiere,
the story that fate had always intended.
And just before the final credits roll,
when your name appears everywhere,
and just before the music swells, and the lights go up,
and everyone in the audience reaches for their hankie,
let this be your final line,
uttered like a suspect out of film noir—
 That's my story,
 and I'm sticking to it.

†

Genesis 101
Bob Frey

The woods are my bailiwick, me and my digging stick,
while lions, tigers, and bears are looking for theirs.
"All you ever do is play peek-a-boo
with a *grundsau*, so I can make a decent stew,
or dangle a stringle in a pool.
We need protein in my hot stone stew;
just turnips, rutabagas, and kale won't do,
and these rocks here hurt my feet.
I think a house would be really neat—
Let's use these rocks to build our castle;
it won't be that much of a hassle."
So, with the rocks laid, a house was made.
"And with this nice bare soil, let's continue our toil.
Now don't panic, we will grow vegetables purely organic."

So he got a bough and built the first chisel plow
and made a harness for his Princess,
so she could pull his newly invented tool
to till their land in manner cool.
But she gave him an ear full—"It's hard to pull, I need an animal."
So, he went down to the equator and got her an alligator.
"The thing won't help feed us and in fact may even eat us!
Take it back like I say, right away, and neither will a kangaroo do."
So he trundled off until he found her a giant sloth,
The behemoth came with moss and mold, really gross.
"What I want is a horse, if one you come across,
a real animal this plow to pull."

15

Rewriting the Past

"If we get a horse a corral is a must,
I know where there is a grove of locust for posts."
Off he went with his stone axe, a hundred-foot tree to attack.
He whacked away the whole day, and it didn't even sway.
He came back with back a-breaking and muscles aching.

Furry pillow talk, deep in thought, "I think we ought
not invent the wheel, bronze, iron, and steel,
and just quit while we are ahead," so he said.
"It's too much for my cranium, let us get some uranium
and blow up the whole shebang, forget about your own Mustang,
and cease the cultivation of our plantation.
We will go back to forest primeval, forget our farming sustainable."
"It's fine with me," said she. "I kept my old digging stickie.
Let us return to the boonies, leave this to the loonies,
and leave poor poems like this, to some other futurist.
And be sure to cut down that apple tree!" Said she.
"But save the fig tree for me."

✝

The Hanger
Robert L. Martin

Rules of time and the chronology of it,
When order was a wondrous piecing together,
As the minutes grew into marvelous hours,
And rudiments advanced to triumphant ends,
They took me and delivered me to my fate.

I stood in awe of my mounted accomplishments,
My integrity beyond a questionable doubt,
My up righteous visions fully ingrained,
The rudiments grabbing a hold and leading me,
Sinking into my spongy mind and electric body,
Becoming me, equipped with all the ingredients,
Taking me up to the summit for my crowning,
With perfection waiting at the top of the mount,
Whispering to the ear of my exhilarated heart,
"Perfection is a dream to be seen,
And an all-out effort to fulfill it.
Failure looms ahead from an effort unfulfilled."

My right arm was an extension of my fortitude,
My insurance that good fortune is mine to inherit,
A dream that became my mechanical reality,
My thoughts that led me to the upper echelon,
My physicality that placed me there,
A reminder that my fingers are all powerful
As they wrap around the baseball,
As my mind takes command of them.

Rewriting the Past

Baseball has never known
A pitcher such as I, destined for
The Hall at Cooperstown, 'Tis me alright.

My changeup keeps the hitters off stride,
Except the hanger that I left over the middle,
The one that challenged McGregor to hit,
The one that swelled up as big as a watermelon,
That hung over the plate waiting for him to hit,
Daring him to knock it out of the park,
The one that grew a mouth
And started trashing him,
"Hit me McGregor, I betcha can't.
Ya-ya-ya-ya-ya."

As McGregor's blood began to boil,
His big ecstatic eyes glued to the ball,
His internal arsenal stocked with TNT,
His muscles ripping through his shirt,
His belly spewing lava out of his mouth,
The earth shaking from his pounding feet,
He swung with all his might
And sent the ball flying through the night.
The loudness of breaking glass
In the parking lot
Woke me from my nervous sleep.
Alas, my dream showed me
How to pitch to him.

As my dream became an admonition
And transported me back to
Change the course of yesterday's game,
I gave that dirtbag McGregor nothing to hit,

Rewriting the Past

Nothing in the strike zone,
No changeups, no hangers, no nothing.
"Whatsa matter, little baby?
Too scared to pitch to me?" He blurted out,
As he walked to first base.
Then Wilson, a 145 hitter,
Struck out to end the game.
Yes, I was scared, but we won the game,
Didn't we? 1-0.
Thanks to my dream last night
And my friendly supernatural counselor
That hated McGregor, too.

✝

My Haven
Beatriz Eugenia Arias

I wake up to the light of day
And envision in my mind
In a place not far away
I wonder what I will find.
Ah! There they are my beauties
Fluttering in all directions
But, I cannot shun my duties
To seek their continuous affection.
This My Haven—My Refuge
That matters to no one
Keeps me from a deluge
Of emotions on the run.
What would the trees 'midst the blue skies
Be like without music—
These birds of all sizes
With such an acoustic.
Had I but known
That this would pass
I would have stood still,
Alas!

✝

Our Future
Kelly Craig Decker

Don't rewrite the past
It was the struggles and pain
That helped me find you

Past Thoughts Reborn
Thornton Blease

Let my words be few
But laced with thunder.

Let my eyes swallow every shard, rusty nail, distorted vision,
Rainbow's tail,
But please, oh please, do not mouth my faintest thoughts . . .

I am no mountain,
I cannot, will not support the sky,
Shoulder the earth and all her woes,
Though I will try . . .

I am no gambler,
No greased-up-sliding fingers,
No creeping whiplash smile . . .

I have no lion's mane, no silver grinning bullet,
No rose smeared daggers underneath my shirt,
No gut-filching vices or strongman virtues . . .

Only thoughts already voiced and hammered brittle,
Bound together, all anew . . .

✝

Would I, Could I, If I Could
Judy England-McCarthy

If I could, would I change the past,
Make it different to the last.
Whirling, twirling life goes by.
If not now, then when, and why?

A glimpse of a young man, our eyes suddenly meet.
A random chance encounter while crossing the street.
Recognition and a bright smile reaches our eyes.
Reflecting happy memories without even a try.
My feelings come back to me in an instant rush.
Suddenly, I'm a girl again with an overwhelming crush.

Some memories I could change,
Many more to rearrange.
What would be first to go,
Perhaps this one, I do not know.

"I do," I say to the minister, come what may,
To create a bond, time cannot wither away.
Out in a farmer's field, our vows were made.
On a bright sunny day so many plans were laid.
Many lifetime possibilities just begun.
When the two of us vowed to live as one.

Rewriting the Past

If I could, would I change the past.
Make it different to the last.
Whirling, twirling life shall go on.
Even if all my past begone.

Push again, one more time and breathe the midwives say.
My darling son, though late, was truly on his way.
Beyond exhausted, with my own mother nearby,
Such joy and happiness I feel, I wish to cry.
Much time has passed and my little boy is far away.
He is grown up now, and is in college this day.

Life goes by the way it should.
Would I, could I, if I could,
Alter what is very vast,
Go back, today and change my past?

Sitting at my desk, wondering this very thing.
I glance down and do chance upon my wedding ring.
If, I think, I do change a moment in my life,
Would I now be here still, a mother and a wife?
Perhaps who we are, is who we were meant to be.
Accepting, not changing the past does set us free.

✝

You Are
Sandra Almonte

You were there.
In that dark place that came into existence.
When I didn't understand,
When I didn't have a voice.

You are there.
In that pit of hell that permeates my memories.
When I want to run away from the pain,
Where no one can see me.

Why are You there?
It doesn't make sense.
You say You will never leave me nor forsake me.
It's so hard to let go and trust.

You are here.
Shattering the darkness with light.
You are not here to change the past,
You are here to mend a chosen vessel.

✝

Short Fiction

Alexander's History
Susan Kling Monroe

History is all in how you view it, thought Alexander Bennett. He viewed himself in the wooden framed mirror on the maple dresser, attempting to Windsor-knot the burgundy tie that Margaret had loved.

"Look at you, Old Man," he said, peering into the glass. Those gnarled fingers were slower now, and the tying took longer, giving him time to examine that elderly stranger in the mirror. Gray hair, short enough in this day and age, but not a buzz cut, or whatever the kids called it now. He was always startled to look at his reflection and see an adult, a retiree, and not the messy-haired boy still ready to climb a backyard tree. Last year, it would have been Margaret fussing over the tie. "Let me do it, love. You always tie it funny," she'd say.

No need for a mirror back then. That was in the past, now. History.

As he tightened the knot and smoothed the fabric, Alex decided that tonight he would experiment with an eating spot that had changed hands three times over the course of the past ten years. Each new owner managed to find a pun that was awful and obvious. How many puns could be made about pizza? At least three. Margaret had loved all of them.

Pizza My Heart, inexpensive, and filled with locals, some who looked only vaguely familiar. They'd liked the quiet here—the fact that there was little chance they'd run into people from work. Now, though, the noise and bustle of a restaurant would make a change from the silence at home. The aroma of tomato and cheese would be heartening. Alex microwaved what he could now, and there was no comparison to the smell and taste of his wife's cooking.

Margaret had passed away after forty years of companionable

29

matrimony. The maple dresser, much of the solid wooden furniture in their small house, had been in her family for years. Every stick of it was a reminder of their life together. They'd planned on doing so much when he retired, only to lose those plans to cancer before Alex had a chance to leave teaching.

He did not know where to start, without Margaret.

If he traveled now, it would be alone. Alone was not just the house full of fading memories empty of any life other than his. Alone meant no racket of chattering students, the flap of paper and pages as they worked, the distinctive clattering drop of pencils, brushed, accidentally or on purpose, from desk tops.

Alexander Bennett missed school. Not the building—a school, much like history, is made up of people. Buildings are merely starting points, providing background and bits of context. School was never about the linoleum floors and tall windows of his echoing, ancient classroom. It was not the smell of chalk dust, or the cool slate board under his fingers. Alex had enjoyed interchanges with colleagues, engaging young minds. He firmly believed that what made the school an entity was that interaction with other human beings. Each of those people had their own story. Their own history within that community.

His teacher friends encouraged him to continue teaching, as a substitute. When that didn't appeal, his last principal—and how many of those had he outlasted—suggested he mentor, or better yet, advise the History Club. His most recent principal, Fred Bart, hadn't been born when Alex started teaching. "You love history, Alex! There are ways you can keep active in the field.

Without answering, Alex had gone home to his empty, quiet house.

And so tonight, Alex went out for supper, preferring noisy anonymity to being alone.

He took a book along. No need to sit and stare at the food, inviting sympathetic glances at the old man eating, unaccompanied. It was a thick, glossy-covered volume on the life of George Washington. A colleague who retired years ago had told him that she was never alone, because she had so many books to catch up on after years of encouraging others to read. Books were like old and new friends. Alex liked to read well enough. He was more of a fact man than a lover of fiction.

His books tended to be marked up with question marks on passages that he wanted to verify, or if necessary, to correct. He knew that just because something was written didn't make it factual or accurate. Just because an event was interpreted one way did not mean that analysis wouldn't continue when forgotten facts came to light. Looking at facts in context was an important distinction he'd always been at pains to pass on to his students.

A product of the 1950s, he had seen many children's works available on the first president. All had started with the tale of George Washington chopping down a cherry tree, of being discovered by his father, and of confessing to the deed in a presidential act of honesty. In those days, cherry pie had been a standard treat on Washington's Birthday.

All false. All written not long after Washington's death by Parson Weems, an eighteenth-century do-gooder seeking to impart a need for honesty in children, and hopefully the adults they would eventually become. Weems's writing then became false history. That story had been Alex's first understanding that the past was sometimes understood incorrectly, and needed to be revisited based on more accurate information. For many years Alex had used those books, and the iconic painting by Grant Wood, to teach selection of resources, about facts versus myth.

His students were, for the most part, respectful. There had been rascals —those he'd never found a way to reach—like Wisniewski. John Wisniewski. Alex would never forget that one.

"History is useless," John commented loudly on one of those last mornings of Alex's career—skinny chest puffed out as the boy showed off for the cheerleader stacking her books next to him, John had continued, "People should just get over their old ways and move on. Let the dead stay dead and not bother the living."

John Wisniewski was wrong. History as a subject was more relevant than ever. Finding the key to sparking interest in each new generation of students had become difficult. Worrying, even. So, while his belief in the field was as passionate as it had ever been, Alex as a purveyor of that passion had felt irrelevant.

Had he ever had the distinction of relevance? He'd mostly been concerned with getting as much background as he could into his students' heads before they went off into the wide world. That framework should be a foundation for comprehending the world at large—*should*, but not always *was*. As the years passed, and more children like John Wisniewski arrived, Alex came to feel his life's work as wasted.

History might be a basis for understanding the world, but football and video-gaming commanded more of the students' hearts. Those students would move on to more important things, like a steady job and place in community, without a backward glance at their old history lessons.

The school district offered early retirement bonuses in an effort to cull the more expensive, long-lived teachers from their September lineup. Heartsick, Alex had chosen to take them up on the offer, if a little too late for Margaret.

Now he was here, at Pizza My Heart. "Damn fool name for a pizza parlor," he told himself. Perhaps it was better if he joined Margaret sooner rather than later?

"Excuse me?"

The elderly man looked up into the tired eyes of the thirty-something waitress who went on to ask, "Do you teach at Columbia High School?"

Her face beneath the streaked blonde hair was familiar. So many faces seemed that way after decades of teaching. Mr. Bennett nodded and offered a smile back, "Yes. I did. I retired this year."

"You were my teacher!" she bubbled. "I'm Sherry. I was Sherry Watson, but now I'm Sherry Dietrich. I married Matt Dietrich. Do you remember us?"

Heaven help him, he did. Not this older, lived-in variation, but the younger, sparkling teenage girl who had written for the school paper. And, Matt Dietrich—he knew the name, but could not call the face to mind. "Are you still writing?" he asked.

That worn face with its bright lipstick lit up, revealing the child she'd once been. "You do remember! Not so much anymore. I did get my journalism degree, but it doesn't really pay around here. And we have kids . . . uh, I should get your order. What would you like?"

His order given, and the restaurant being quiet for a Tuesday night, the old man ignored the book under his hand. He deliberated, exhuming rusty social skills as he waited for Sherry to return with a tall glass of unsweetened iced tea, cool droplets condensing on the sides.

"What is Matt doing now?" Alex lobbed back in the usual conversational volley.

"Matt's a truck driver for the quarry. It's a union job. It pays well. I make a little extra money here to build up a travel fund."

That was interesting. "Where do you travel?" he asked with more than polite interest.

"Well, it *is* your fault. Do you remember when you had that Minuteman come in to talk to the class?"

Alex remembered. A friend, someone he'd not spoken to in years now, standing tall at the front of the room wearing the heavy woolen uniform and stout leather shoes of the Continental Congress. No Brown Bess of course—no guns allowed in school. Not technically a "minuteman," but he said, "Ah, yes. Samuel Adams." In his talk with the classes, Sam had made much of the fact that the original Founding Father with his name had not served on the front lines.

Sherry grinned. "After Matt and I got married, we visited a cousin in New Jersey. He dragged us to the Tempe Wick house near the old Washington encampment in Morristown. They had men dressed the same way, giving tours. Matt started talking to them. He never forgot the stuff we learned in your class. We've been visiting battlefields and National Historical sites ever since. Matt calls it 'Visiting History.' He says history needs to be talked about. It needs to be part of our lives for it to be of any use."

Alex discovered himself smiling broadly, a flash of joy warming him. "I told him that. He remembered."

"We both do. And we share it with our sons. The kids pretend they're bored, but they've been acing their social studies classes, so we figure it's a win."

"I'm glad to hear that. It's excellent that you're sharing history with your children." Mr. Bennet could not have stopped himself from grinning.

His meal, when it came, was made all the better by this stirring of the mud his memories had become. Teaching was so much more than a lecture, or tests out of textbooks. Or the John Wisniewskis of the world. There had been bright faces, interested questions, joy in learning as well as frustration. Book ignored, Alex enjoyed his eggplant Parmesan, thinking instead of Italy —the brick structure of the pizza joint itself dredged up memories of the waves of immigrants, the Great Arrival of the 19th century, and then the war brides from World War II. And those memories led into that of Margaret's excitement about someday visiting the Eternal City of Rome.

That painting on the wall, he thought. *A barefoot woman in a peasant dress following a donkey up a mountain side. It's probably the least accurate or connected artifact in the room. Perpetuates our stereotypes.* Those were the kinds of things he liked to discuss with his students. Italy had been only one of the places that he and Margaret planned to travel in retirement.

He thanked Sherry on his way out. "It was wonderful to see you. Please give my regards to Matt. And keep talking about history with your boys!"

In the morning, over his cup of coffee, he found himself staring past the shelf of biographies into his own past.

His teaching, his work, had made a difference in Sherry and Matt's lives, even their family's life—a real difference.

Alex expected to be forgotten, along with the subject he'd taught. Alex had written off his own past as a life misspent. If his lifetime had not been wasted, then perhaps there was work for him to do yet.

The phone felt unusual in his hand. The number he dialed—such an old-fashioned word. What should it be now? Entered? The entered number was familiar. "Hello. May I speak with Mr. Bart, please? Thank you."

"Fred? It's Alex Bennett. No, nothing is wrong. Yes, still retired. Have you found an adviser for the History Club yet? And I've been thinking about a Sophomore field trip to Gettysburg . . ."

✝

The Decision
Phyllis Palamaro

Blanche was thirty when she became pregnant with her second child. Wasn't really her choice. Her life had been good, carefree, with much independence. Her daughter, Phillie, was almost nine, an easy, obedient child. Her husband Eddie was a good provider, but fifteen years older than she. He was from Poland and very old school about what she could and could not do.

Eddie's wife didn't work.

Damn his pride! She gave up a good job as a secretary to marry him. That was a mistake. There were other things she wanted to do, places she would have liked to see. Eddie, on the other hand, enjoyed television after work, watching baseball games—the New York Yankees, the Brooklyn Dodgers. So boring! She enjoyed listening to opera on the radio and watching ballet on television.

Blanche had never learned how to fight for what she wanted. Eddie wanted a son, but she felt trapped and imagined the boredom and loneliness of caring for an infant. All in their thirties, none of her friends were expecting.

I can't do this again.

Blanche couldn't talk to Eddie about her feelings. He would shut down and look uncomfortable. "Isn't a paycheck enough?" he would grumble. Her older sister, Anna, had two adopted sons and seemed jealous of her pregnancy. Her younger sister had two daughters and her accounting job, but no time for talking about feelings. "What's the big deal?" Beth would say. "Get on with it."

Blanche's mother, Esther, lived with Anna. Mom was from Europe and,

36

like her husband, had no time for feelings. She was a lot like Eddie, but with more heart. What a mess!

Where was a friend when she needed one?

I can't do this, Blanche repeated to herself. She pictured herself broken in spirit, alone, nonfunctional. She feared a nervous breakdown. Then what would happen? She would be placed in a "home." Everyone would change.

Life would be so hard for Eddie, Phillie, and the baby. Esther would have to come and care for all of them.

Blanche would return a different person. Loud, demanding, and overbearing, she would dislike her husband, daughter, and son.

Most of all she would dislike herself.

She would hate her life.

No! I won't let this happen. I'll make Eddie get a nurse to help me. I'll love this little one, and not play off the kids against each other. I'll kill them with kindness. Somewhere I read, "Acceptance brings peace." I will accept this child.

So it began.

Henry's birth was not an easy one. Eddie was proud of the boy, but Blanche had to work hard to like him. The nurse, Emma, came in every day. She was good with the baby and Phillie. Blanche had at least some of her free time back. She could go for walks, meet friends for lunch, and have her hair done. Slowly, Emma placed more and more of the baby's care into Blanche's hands. Without realizing it, Blanche eventually became the mother she wanted to be.

When Henry was three months old, Emma left for another assignment. Blanche was still shaky, but allowed Phillie to care for her little brother when she came home from school. Eddie barely held his son and refused to change diapers. Phillie became her mother's ally. "Go for a walk, mom. I'll watch Hen." Eddie never realized the bond developing between his wife and daughter.

Time marched on.

ᔰ

Phillie was 22 and married. Henry was 13 and hung around Blanche too much. He needed to be more independent. Blanche encouraged him to make friends. She found ways of not being home when he returned from school. Eddie considered her negligent.

Then Henry was drafted into the army and thought his world had ended. Blanche was afraid for him, but also relieved. He threatened to desert to Canada. Eddie was furious. So Henry entered the army and survived. He found that he had computer science skills and earned a degree with his GI bill. He was recommended for a job in Manhattan by Phillie's husband. He made good use of his computer skills, advancing in his job, but never moved out of his parents' apartment. He found it hard to cut the apron strings.

After Eddie retired, he and Blanche moved to Florida. Henry wanted to go with them, but Blanche discouraged him and Eddie backed her up. He remained in the Brooklyn apartment, a bit lost and lonely at first. Eventually, he made friends, and finally married a girl when he was in his thirties.

Blanche never liked Paula, her daughter-in-law. She was pushy and seemed to boss Henry around, but the grandkids were wonderful and visited often.

Blanche's granddaughter, Helen, wanted to be a nurse, and deliberately chose a school in Florida, close to her nana. Eddie had died six years before, and Helen visited whenever she could take time from her nursing studies.

One day, Helen asked, "Grandma, what's it like to be married and have children?"

"Helen, darling, life is all about choices and attitude. When your father was born, I had a decision to make. I was never sorry I made it. Grab life and enjoy it. Change what you can. Never lose who you are for someone else." Helen heard Blanche's story. She didn't repeat it to her mother. She vowed she would never marry a man fifteen years her senior even though she had loved her grandfather. She thought her father a weak but kindly man.

Her prince charming would be strong and not bossy. She also would be strong. She would be a good nurse. Paula would care for her strong, honest, brave Nana Blanche for as long as she could. Regardless of what her mother said about her!

❧

This is the history of when my mother had my brother. I rewrote and fictionalized it so that my mother realized she had a choice and made the decision to get help with the newborn so that she could raise the child and care for her family in a positive way. It would have changed the lives of my whole family.

✝

The Encounters
Gail Brittenburg

The kitchen was quiet except for the clink of the forks, spoons, and knives dropping into the drawer. My fifteen-year-old sister, Kathy, washed the dishes. I dried.

Drying had been my job since I was seven, maybe earlier. At fourteen it seemed like forever. Kathy's hands played in the suds. She had fun . . . I was jealous. Once, when I was eleven, I asked my stepmother if I could wash instead of dry.

"No! You'll cut yourself with a knife or break a glass," she snapped.

I mumbled, "Stop pretending you care." I never asked again.

Our other sister, Linda, seventeen, graduated from high school and a few months later got a job at a slip cover company within walking distance of the house. Linda was thrilled to earn money, and the freedom and happiness it promised.

The plates clattered on the shelf as I stacked them. When I reached to set the last dish, I heard a loud angry voice. Startled, I dropped the plate and it shattered on the floor.

"Who do you think you're talking to?" exploded from the other room. Our house was small. There were only two rooms on the first floor, the kitchen and living room. Kathy and I ventured one step, then another, inching our bodies toward the archway. We peeked in.

Who's he screaming at?

My dad's yell increased in volume. "As long as you are living under our roof, we want money for room and board!"

"No! It's my money!" Linda shouted back. "I wanna save for a car!" Her

40

voice retreated with a quiver, "Room and board, for this prison?"

A slap and shove silenced Linda's pleas. Her body flew across the room. She hit the wall hard, bounced off, and collapsed to the floor.

My eyes blurred with tears and my leg muscles tightened as I watched. Kathy and I stood powerless. All we could do was witness Linda's one and only brave moment.

Her limp beanpole body shook with fear as she crouched on the floor. Her chin trembled but she wouldn't give Dad the satisfaction of crying. A deep red mark, the size of his hand, covered the left side of her face.

"Get up off the floor and go to your room!" he demanded.

Our father was as round as he was short, but as scary as Godzilla.

Linda peeled herself off the floor.

His blazing eyes followed her every move as she stumbled toward the steps, until he spotted Kathy and me. His nostrils flared and his eyes bulged when he realized he had an audience.

Our cheeks were drenched with tears. We held our breath. Our bodies squirmed as if we were next, which only infuriated him even more.

"What are you looking at?" he bellowed. "What are you crying about? Get upstairs!"

We couldn't move fast enough. Kathy pushed herself ahead of me. I pulled then pushed her back. We bolted to the third floor. Linda was already on her bed whimpering with her back toward us. She pretended to be asleep. I gently touched her shoulder and without a word climbed into my bed. Sleep didn't come easy.

Our attic bedroom had one little window facing the front of the house. The window was painted shut. Three twin beds lined the opposite wall. My sisters and I were confined to the attic around the clock unless we were in school or doing chores.

The door didn't have a lock to hold us captive, but we learned from a young age not to go downstairs, let alone open the door, unless told.

Six-thirty the next morning, Kathy and I awoke and got ready for school. Linda's bed was empty as usual. She began work at six.

It took us fifteen minutes flat to get dressed. We sat and waited for our stepmother, Marie, to give the command. She'd call from the bottom of the steps: "Kathy and Gail . . . get down here for breakfast!"

Soldier style, we descended toward the kitchen to devour our meager breakfast of corn flakes. She must have poured the milk in the bowl ten minutes before she called because the cereal was already mushy. That's not a great way to start a day.

You'd think at our age we'd be able to make our own breakfast.

Marie stood watch like a prison guard as she wrote a grocery list of stuff she'd need to make dinner. She kept one eye on us and guarded the trash can. If we attempted to toss the cereal and refill the bowl, she'd pull our hair.

When I was finished eating, she'd hand me the list. It was my job to walk the few long alleys to the corner market on Main Street.

Tess and Newton were the owners. They had white hair and were happy to see me every morning. Kathy did the breakfast dishes while I was gone. When I returned, I placed the groceries on the kitchen table for Marie's inspection.

When our stepmother dismissed us, we grabbed our books and walked to school.

The high school was five blocks up, and three blocks to the left. I was more a socializer than student. Kathy, on the other hand, excelled in the honors group.

At the day's end the two of us would meet at a side door and walk the twenty minutes home.

"I wonder if Linda's face was still red this morning." Kathy said as she skipped over the cracks on the sidewalk.

"I don't know," I replied, trying to keep up with her. "If it was, her friends at work are gonna ask her what happened."

As we reached the door of our house, a faint argument interrupted our conversation. Our parents' voices, now louder, could be heard through the walls.

Should we go in? What happened?

The swearing stopped for a second. I hesitated but turned the knob. The instant our feet touched the carpet we faced a firing squad of questions.

"Do you know where your sister is? Did you know she left? Who is she with?" My father hollered.

Scared, we shook our heads side to side.

Standing in the middle of the room he babbled about Linda's boss checking to see if she was sick . . . she didn't show up for work . . . he checked her closet and her clothes were gone.

He turned to us again. "Don't you two get any ideas of doing the same! I don't want her name mentioned in this house," he ranted as he ripped Linda's 8x10 graduation picture off the wall. "Get upstairs," he screeched.

Music to our ears! We tripped on our feet as we ran to oblige him.

Kathy and I looked at the closet. Linda's half was empty. She was gone! We tried to piece together what happened. "She must have put all her clothes in a bag and left. Did she go last night or did she go this morning?" Kathy smiled a slight grin.

"I'm glad she escaped. I don't blame her. Who do they think they are?" Kathy said in a hostile voice. "We'll go too someday, they'll be sorry."

The room felt empty and cold. The screaming continued downstairs.

Our sister was gone. Her name was never spoken again in our parents' presence. We didn't hear from her and had no idea what happened. Her sheets were removed from her bed and it stood naked. Kathy and I lived day by day with the mystery of Linda always on our minds.

Two years passed with no word from Linda. Kathy was preparing for graduation.

Mine would be next year. It was Thursday and we had a half day of school. A few blocks from Liberty High, Kathy and I turned toward the frantic string of beeps from a blue car parked along the curb. A woman with a striped head band emerged.

"Oh my God, it's Linda!" Kathy shrieked with excitement.

"Linda!" I cried with joy.

Linda ran with her arms stretched wide to give us a hug.

"Mom is not dead! They lied to us!" Linda blurted.

"She's not?" Kathy yelled as she choked on her gum. "How do you know?"

"You know Tess and Newton from the grocery store? They're our grandparents! They told me right before I graduated." Linda said breathless. "They told me all about Mom and how she wants to be a part of our life. They gave me her phone number."

"Did you talk to her?" I stammered. "Did you meet her? What's she like?"

"She's wonderful! When I left home, I called her. We spent the day together and she helped me figure out what to do and where to go," Linda said, elated. "She helped me find an apartment and paid for my first month's rent."

"Kathy, next week you graduate, here's her number. She really wants to meet all of us," Linda said. "Call her."

"I can't . . . I can't leave Gail home alone. She'll get stuck there. She'll be afraid without me and won't have the guts to leave. I'll wait a year until she graduates and we'll leave together." Kathy sighed. "Tell Mom so she doesn't look for me."

"We better get home," Kathy turned away. "They'll wanna know why we're late."

"Okay! I'll let Mom know. Stay safe," Linda said as she slid back into the car.

We ran the few blocks home and stumbled through the door. Through the kitchen window, we could see our stepmother sweeping the porch.

Whew! She didn't see us.

With shaky laughter, we climbed the steps to our room.

We sat on the edge of the bed. "This is amazing," Kathy said, her voice choked with emotion. "All we have to do is survive one more year. Can you

44

hold on?"

I gripped Kathy's hand. "Yep, just one more year. Thanks for waiting for me," I said, tearing up. "I can't believe Mom's alive and wants to see us."

For the next twelve months we flinched, cringed, and obeyed to avoid any danger that would ruin our plan of escape. We wished for the year to fly quickly so our dreams could come true sooner. Our wish came true.

Time passed . . . My graduation was now just a week away. Our plan of escaping Dad was set. Linda would park a block away and wait for us on Saturday morning. The routine for Saturday was for us to wash the kitchen floor, vacuum, dust, and do laundry while our parents slept in . . . but not today. They'll be surprised!

It was time! With a sweaty hand I opened the door and watched it close behind us for the last time.

Nauseous, we held our bags of clothes, fled to Linda's waiting car, and drove off.

Ten minutes later Linda pulled into a driveway. The large contemporary rancher sat on a huge lot with overgrown trees.

"Here we are! Your turn to meet Mom." Linda said. She kept the car idling as we scooted out the back seat. She then drove away.

Kathy and I stood and stared at the yellow door with skinny windows on each side.

A moment later, the door opened. A beautiful blond haired woman wearing a flowery dress stepped out. Her sad, yet happy face told me this wasn't easy for her either. The woman smiled, and my soul filled with a marvelous peace. She walked toward us.

"Hello," she said. "I'm Betty, your mother." She reached to give us a squeeze. The soft touch embraced my heart. I was home!

We hugged, cried, and excitedly talked while we strolled toward the house. Her husband, George, met us at the door. His stature was strong, and his gray temples softened his face with kindness.

Our mother motioned for us to sit at the dining room table. She took a deep breath and began to say everything she'd been wanting to say for years.

Rewriting the Past

"I'm so sorry you were led to believe I died," Betty apologized. "I was heartbroken when I had to leave you girls. The choice was not mine. Without a job, I couldn't give you three a decent home or provide for you." She seemed embarrassed.

Two hours into our sharing, forgiving, and understanding the phone rang.

"Hello." George answered.

"Are my daughters there?" my father barked.

"Yes," George said calmly.

"You tell those brats they are no longer my daughters! They are dead to me!" he shouted.

"Sure, feelings are mutual!" George growled as he slammed the phone down.

He walked into the kitchen and with a quick smile he announced, "Well, your father won't be bothering you anymore."

In the evening, Betty prepared our beds. It was a long day; we were exhausted. Once our heads hit the pillow, we fell asleep within a minute.

The months that followed were like heaven. Our mother wanted our dreams to be fulfilled.

Kathy's desire was to be a nurse. Betty encouraged her to enroll at a nursing school and offered to pay the tuition. Kathy applied at St. Luke's Nursing School and became a nurse at an esteemed hospital.

My desire was to learn the mechanics of appliances, how they worked, and how to do repairs. I applied and got accepted into Lincoln Tech, the highest ranking school in the area.

My goal was to own and operate my own laundromat. George and my mother had faith in me therefore; after graduation they helped me purchase a laundromat in a college town.

George did the finances for the business, and Mom helped me decorate the laundromat with an "at home" feel.

Kathy and I eventually met and married wonderful husbands and blessed Betty with grandchildren.

But! . . . The ending written above never happened. It was my "if dreams could come true" version of meeting my mother when I was eighteen.

The truth was a far cry from my expectations. When Betty met us, after all those years, "blessed" is not how she felt. We were a reminder of the sadness she tried to escape during her lifetime. After her death, we discovered Betty had suppressed a shocking, shameful secret.

However, that's another story to be written—or rewritten.

✝

Gertie Rewrites Her Life
Thornton Blease

Near the end of her life, she had cultivated African violets, and had a cheerful room that she filled with flowers. She had learned how to grow the most extravagant strains, which she liked to give as gifts so everybody had in their homes an inescapable reminder of Gertie.

She died surrounded by inconsolable relatives, reposed in her fashionable fuchsia silk robe. In her final hours, she had been overcome with enormous disappointment because life had not granted her more than eighty-six years. No one knew why she never tired of living; she had worked like a mule for almost all of her life. But that older generation had something that made them more resilient. Like all earlier things—the cars, the watches, the lamps, the chairs, the plates and pots of yesteryear—Gertie, too, had been made of stronger stuff . . .

❧

Gertie had, like all of her sisters, long thin legs, broad shoulders, and a hard smile. She was the daughter of a physician, a wise and fascinating man who filled life with his taste for music, art, and poetry. However, as fates like to even the score, Gertie had more than enough father, but less than enough husband. She fell in love and married a man named Herbert whose only defect was that he was so much like his children that Gertie had to treat him like one. He wasn't much good at earning money, and the idea that men should support their families, so common in the 1950s, didn't govern his existence. To put food on the table and buy blankets for the beds, to clothe the children and pay for their schooling—not to mention the rest of life's expenses—was solely up to his devoted and acquiescing wife, Gertie.

Meanwhile, Herbert schemed up big business deals that he never pulled off. To close one of these deals, he had the brilliant idea of writing a check on nonexistent funds for a sum so large that a warrant was issued for his arrest, and the police arrived at the house to take him away.

When Gertie learned of this, she said the first thing that popped into her mind. "What's happened is that this man is crazy. Totally nuts."

With this line of reasoning, she accompanied him to his trial; with this line of reasoning, she kept him from mounting his own defense; and with this line of reasoning, she kept him from being thrown in jail. Instead, Gertie arranged for Herbert to be committed to a mental hospital near the Delaware Water Gap. It was a tranquil place at the foot of the hills, run by the Sisters of The Sacred Heart of Jesus.

Grateful for the medical visits of Gertie's father, the Sisters agreed that Herbert could stay until the incident with the check was forgotten. Of course, Gertie had to pay for the monthly care of that sane man within the impregnable walls of the mental ward. For six months, she made every effort to cover the cost of his stay and visit him faithfully every Friday at noon. When her finances could stretch no further, she decided to retrieve her husband after first having herself declared his legal guardian.

One Sunday she went to get him in Blairstown. She found him breakfasting among the brothers that supervised his unit, entertaining them with a tale about a sailor who had a mermaid tattooed on the bald spot on top of his head.

"One wouldn't look bad on you, Brother John," he said to the one with the biggest smile.

While Herbert was talking, he watched his wife coming down the corridor. He and the brothers continued joking and laughing with that childish joy that men only seem to have when they know they're among themselves.

As if unaware of the rules of such a gathering, Gertie walked around the table in the clickety-clacking high heels she wore on important occasions. When she was in front of her husband, she greeted the group with a smile.

"What are you doing here?" Herbert asked, more uncomfortable than surprised.

"I came to get you." Gertie spoke as she did to her children when she met them at school, pretending to trade their freedom in exchange for a hug.

Herbert was clearly annoyed. "Why? I'm safe here. It's not time for me to leave. What's more, I'm having a good time. There's an aura of peace here that does wonders for my spirit."

Gertie narrowed her eyes at him. "What?"

"I'm said I'm fine right here where I am. Don't worry. I have some good, sane friends and I don't get along badly with the loonies. Some of them have moments of exceptional inspiration; others are eloquent speakers. The rest has done me good, because in this place even the screamers make less noise than your kids." As if he had nothing to do with the existence of their children.

"Herbert, what am I going to do with you?" Gertie shook her head as she turned toward the exit. She whispered to the nun accompanying her. "Please, Sister, can you explain to him that his vacations cost money? I'm not going to pay for one day more."

One can only guess what the nun told Herbert, but the following Monday morning, the latch on Gertie's front door made a slow sound—the same leisurely noise it used to make when her husband pushed it open.

"I came home, Mother," Herbert said with a mourner's sadness.

Gertie showed no surprise. "That's good, Son. Mr. Hoffler is waiting to see you."

"To offer me a business deal." His voice recovered some liveliness. "You'll see what a deal, Gertie. This time you'll see."

～

"And that's the way the man was," Gertie commented many years later. "All his life was like that."

By then, Gertie's bed and breakfast had become a success and had provided her with enough profit to expand her business as well as support Herbert's disastrous money-making schemes. She used her earnings to open a restaurant, which she closed some time later to get into real estate, and which gave her the opportunity to buy land in New York and some more in the Caribbean.

After Herbert's death at seventy-six years old, Gertie learned how to paint the waves and spill her inner soul through poetry. Few people had been as happy as she was then, finally living life to the fullest.

That is why life really infuriated her, leaving her just when she was beginning to enjoy it.

†

He's Back
Bernadette Sukley

T he kids trudged in.

Rachel felt an electric tingle on the tops of her forearms. *Oh no!* The candle flames in the pumpkin flickered. Bad. Wrong. Awful. *Schlecht.*

The Cinderella, every inch bedecked with flounces, and the slender boy dressed as a soldier handed over their barely filled trick-or-treat bags. Rachel let the bags droop to the floor. The children stood in front of her, heads bowed.

"Back so soon?" she asked, keeping her voice soft to mask her alarm.

Silence.

Oh yes, something bad had happened.

"Sorry Mom," Corey apologized. "He just popped out and . . ." He stopped speaking and sighed. His forlorn gaze drifted to the bags on the floor.

Rachel turned to her daughter "What happened?" She knelt down and put her hands on the girl's rosy cheeks, cooled by the October chill.

Her sweet little face was so sorrowful. But Courtney said nothing, only sniffled, real tears gathered in her eyes.

"It can't be that bad," Rachel soothed her daughter. "It'll be okay."

Courtney shook her head. A tiny dangling pearl on her tiara atop her blond ringlets trembled.

Rachel turned to her son. "Oh, Corey, what did you do?"

Corey pointed to his little sister. "Wasn't me this time, Mom. It was her!"

Courtney found her voice. "I couldn't help it. I just got scared. He just, just . . ." she whimpered and then paused, her lower lip quivered.

Rachel looked back at her son, silent appeal in her eyes.

Corey scooped up the bags and emptied them on the kitchen table. "Here, look Mom, you'll see."

Rachel visually sifted through the small piles of candy. No toads, snakes or anything out of the ordinary. Only blessedly normal name-brand candy. Then a Snickers bar twitched, M&Ms bags slithered aside and a small dark head poked up. Hands and feet followed. A dark-suited man stood on a KitKat bar waving a small fist. His face was angry, very angry. Even his voice, a barely audible squeaking, sounded threatening.

"Oh no!" Rachel groaned.

"Mommy, I'm so, so sorry," Courtney sobbed.

Rachel acted quickly. "No worries, sweetheart," she said brightly. She handed Corey her cellphone. "Call Aunt Leah. We're going to need, uh, help," she whispered the last word.

"Oh Mommy," Courtney wailed. "He, he tried to hurt us!"

Rachel hugged her little girl. "It's okay sweetheart, we'll figure this out."

"Worst day ever," Corcy mumbled. He handed the phone back to Rachel.

Rachel barely said two words before Leah was in full froth. "I don't know why you don't send them to the academy. Courtney can't control her power and Corey doesn't even want to use his anymore after last year!"

Rachel was stung. Single and struggling with two gifted children. She tried to preserve what little innocence they had left. Yes, the Dark was attracted to her children, but it was a back-handed compliment in a way. If your kids were full-knowledged, it didn't pursue them. It was too late by then. Its only goal was to rid the world of that-which-was-not-the-Dark. It did so only by harassing those children unaware of its wiles. It fed them lies and ruined their innocence. Exposed them to its stain, promised conjuring but stole their joy. Never mentioned consequences. Made them grow up too fast and stole their childhood.

Yes, she should have warned Corey before his tenth birthday party not to accept candy from a sneaky goblin. It frightened everyone, except him. There was a lot of explaining—lying—to be done. Guests had to be convinced it was a robotic toy hissing, snarling and noshing birthday cake. When that didn't work, Leah had to reset memories with spells she hadn't used in decades.

"Leah, please, just shut up and come over."

"I'm already in the car," Leah snapped. "A call from you on Halloween? Of course you're in trouble! And of course you need me to come over and fix it!"

Rachel ran to her room and hauled out a large blue leather book from under her bed. She flipped through the pages, passed the recipes for herbal concoctions, and turned to the heavy, creased pages in the back. She recognized the symbols and murmured a few syllables. *Maybe she could get a head start before Leah . . .*

"Mom?" Corey stood at her bedroom door. He gulped. "I don't think that's going to help." He pointed to the book in her hands.

"Why not?" She asked. "We'll just get the man back to normal size, and . . ." She paused. The electric tingle had returned. Bad. Awful. *Schlecht.*

Corey took his mother's hand from the book and led her back to the kitchen table. Courtney was standing guard over the little man heaving Starbursts and Smarties in the air. Rachel saw that his clothing was from another era. With that ugly haircut, stupid moustache, skinny tie and bright red patches on the upper parts of his sleeves, he's certainly not a neighbor. *Phew!*

But oh, how he was cursing. *What a potty mouth!* She listened closely. Nasty German words were directed at her daughter. *Gör! Hurensohn!*

"Why you disgusting little . . ." Her Germanic heritage slipped out, telling him something akin to "feed you to the cat."

"Mom, um, it's a little more complicated," Corey interrupted. "We were by the portal."

"No! How many times have I told you to stay away!" Rachel yelled. She ran her hands through her hair. She inhaled and exhaled slowly, but couldn't keep the panic out of her voice. "Why did you go near it? Remember the first time you saw it? It was weird, right? People showing up out if the blue? All people need to stay where they are in time! You knew it was wrong. We've talked about this Corey." *Hurry up, Leah!*

"Mom, it wasn't our fault, it. It moved! Plus, Courtney's right—he just popped out and grabbed us. He was shaking us. She screamed and then, you know, *poof*. He shrunk. I put him in her bag and we came home," he explained.

"I said, never, never go near . . ." she never finished her sentence.

"Mom! Corey's telling the truth, the portal moved! It's on Oak Street now," Courtney replied with an extra wide pout.

Rachel put a hand to her head. Bad. Awful. *Schrecklich.*

"Hey, maybe we don't need to bring him back to full size." A crooked smile appeared on Corey's face. "Maybe we keep him, like a pet or something?"

"No, Corey! We are sending him back exactly as he was," Rachel was adamant. The time portal had been Corey's favorite temptation. A fluke in the anti-vortex spell caused it to follow gifted children—never too close, but never too far. Corey poked at its silvery surface years ago and out popped Martin Luther. "*Süsses kind!*" He poked Corey, who giggled. He bowed to open-mouthed Rachel and stepped backwards, dissolving into mist. Whispers of, "*Ich bin Martin Luther . . .*" hung in the air, mesmerizing Corey and astounding Rachel. She hustled Corey and baby Courtney away.

Later, she consulted Leah who could offer nothing more than, "I don't know . . . do the anti-vortex spell again?" On his way to school, Corey happened upon a disoriented Albert Einstein, and brought him in to the fourth grade's career day. Fortunately, Einstein's English was so heavily accented no one understood him and laughed at his attempts to use the classroom's SmartBoard. Rachel, homeroom mom extraordinaire, had guided Mr. Einstein back to the blurry hole, given a gentle push and with a subtle shimmer she watched him disappear.

"Back to normal size and then back into the portal. Understood?"

"Uh, Mom," Corey stammered.

"What?"

"Mom, he called himself Adolf Hitler," Corey whispered. "Do we send him back?"

✝

Incorrigible
Judy DeCarlo

News clipping from the Scranton Times dated Sept. 29, 1917:

Youngster leaps from bathroom window of a moving
train and escapes. Andrew Chuck and three other
boys were being transported by a Jersey Central
train to a reformatory in Glen Mills near
Philadelphia. All boys charged with being
incorrigible.

T he boys, along with their guard, stood waiting. They were set to board the 9 a.m. steam locomotive passenger coach, Jersey Central Line. The teens clutched packets stuffed with the story of their offenses. Andrew Chuck, Edward Kowalski, Henry Broman, and Patrick O'Reilly: four boys all headed in the same direction. Out.

Eddie's limbs shook. Patrick spoke with a staccato of stutters while Hank's dread was masked by a sour face and nasty tongue. Meanwhile, Andrew Chuck showed no fear. His demeanor was calm and his stance casual. They might be sending him to the Glen Mills Reformatory School, but he wasn't there yet.

The Scranton train station was the fanciest place Andrew had ever seen and he tried to memorize every ornate detail. The Delaware Western Railroad had spared no expense. Months back, his mother had showed him the *Scrantonian* article. With awe in her voice she'd said the station's walls were constructed of marble imported from Italy, that the floors were tiled in an intricate mosaic and that the ceiling was graced with Tiffany stained glass. Maybe someday he could tell her that, yes, it was as grand as they said.

Concentrating on his surroundings also meant less time to think, less time to observe his fellow travelers. One glance at them and Andrew knew everything. It was in their hungry eyes, discolored teeth, and bruised knuckles. In shirts too loose and britches too tight. In worn shoes and grimy caps, scrawny limbs and forced bravado. It was the dirty hands gripping their Glen Mills Reformatory School folders all stamped with the same damning word: INCORRIGIBLE.

The boys' guardian, Paul Fox, struggled to keep the gawking boys corralled in single file. He had his truants lined up close to the marble wall and quiet, as out of sight as possible, the equivalent of steerage passengers on an ocean liner.

"All aboard!" the call rang through the station.

The boys, as instructed, boarded the train first with heavy reluctant footsteps. Fox barked as he shoved them. "To the back!"

Shackled ankle to ankle, the boys moved as one. "And if anyone needs to do their business, we visit the lavatory now, before decent folks board."

"I gotta go," Hank muttered.

"All right. I'll unfasten your irons but don't try anything funny."

Andrew turned his head to read the man's badge. *P. Fox.* His imagination hummed: *P . . . P . . . the letter P—What first name started with P? Peter Penguin Peanut Brain?* A smile graced his lips. His last teacher called him "mentally deficient" but she didn't know what swam around in his brain.

"What are you grinning about, idiot?" Fox slapped Andrew hard on the back. "And hurry up in there," he called into the latrine. "You got a problem with your plumbing?"

"It's hard to go with everybody looking," Hank complained.

"No one's looking at your sorry pecker," the guard said.

Another good P word, Andrew thought.

"Maybe I didn't need to go after all," Hank said. The others stood silently in the narrow corridor, waiting for instruction. Their eyes were cast downward, where cruel yellow sunshine cast ribbons onto the scuffed floor.

A crisp ruffle of wind from the opened window of the men's water closet breezed over their heads. It hinted of freedom.

"That's it. Show's over. Back to the last bench with you boys and stay quiet. I'll be watching and if there's any sign of trouble . . ." The guard raised his fist but as he did, his left arm begin to tremble, and a prominent tic got his lip pulsing. Even so, he glared at them with mean black eyes.

Andrew read cowardice under Fox's condescension but he had to acknowledge the truth. He and the others were like parcels to be delivered. Cow-like, he demurred as the guard shackled Hank and him together again. Stumbling and awkward, they made their way to their seats, a wooden bench with no cushion.

Moments later, the floodgates of respectability opened and a stream of men, women, and well-dressed children boarded the carriage. Methodically the passengers stowed parcels, removed caps and bonnets, and took their seats. A waft of cherry pipe smoke, hair pomade, and soft lavender perfume filled the air—foreign scents to Andrew, but not unpleasant.

He shifted on the hard wooden bench. His section of the train provided no window but a sudden jolt and hum beneath his feet meant they were moving. There was nothing to distract him but the packet of papers on his lap and the fact that the guard had shut his eyes. Speaking quietly, he nudged his seatmate Hank. "Know what this means?" Andrew pointed at the bold *INCORRIGIBLE* stamp. "The same word's on your folder. I noticed it's on all of ours."

"I can't read long words," Hank said flatly.

Andrew longed to scratch his ankle where the shackle chafed his skin. He envied Hank his thick woolen farm socks but not his inability to read. Without books Andrew couldn't imagine living. His mother used to take him to the Albright Library every other week.

"Incorrigible's the word. I think I'm pronouncing it right. Teachers say that about me. I guess it's why they're sending me off."

"It's 'cause your parents don't want you," Hank accused.

Eddie piped up from across the aisle. "Mine are too poor. They want me."

"That explain your shiner?" Andrew asked and immediately regretted it,

"They c-c-call me n-n-names and I know it's b-b-bad but so what?" Patrick sputtered.

Eddie nodded at the word on his envelope. "I don't know if they call me that. I can't hear so good out this side of my head." He pointed to his left ear, noticeably swollen and not a little misshapen. "So maybe they do."

Eddie hesitated and pointed toward the guard, pantomiming sleep. "I'm glad he's snoring away. I wanted to talk to you guys about that school. I heard them say it's our last chance."

"They say lots of things," Hank spat. "Who cares? They got the chance they wanted. Getting rid of us here on this train." Hank frowned and hooked his thumb into a loop of his overalls. He was the largest of the four, raised on a farm out in Bailey Hollow.

Andrew raked a thin hand through his greasy black hair. He could smell his own unwashed skin. "C'mon, back to that word. Somebody's gotta know what incorrigible means. If it wasn't for that . . ."

Patrick shook his head. "M-m-maybe means we ain't got c-c-courage?"

"Who needs courage?" Hank shot back. "What I need is to piss."

Andrew sighed. While he pitied Hank's discomfort, he despised his resignation. Courage was one thing he knew he needed most to live the kind of life he planned. He learned that from books like *Robinson Crusoe* and *Treasure Island,* and the Longfellow poem, *The Midnight Ride of Paul Revere.*

Andrew noticed the train had slowed, rocking up a steep ascent over a nameless Pennsylvania mountain. Here was opportunity. It wasn't an impulsive move, quite the opposite. It was predestined and necessary.

Andrew had noticed the window in the men's washroom was plenty big. He'd snuck through narrower openings plenty of times before running from shopkeepers or his father. Too bad he had to go it alone, he'd like the company of quiet Eddie or sweet, stuttering Patrick. Maybe even strapping

Hank.

No, all the true heroes did it alone. He was strong enough and smart. Andrew waved his hand, seeking the attention of the now wide-eyed P. Fox

"Whaddya want?" the guard called.

"Need the shitter," Andrew mouthed the words.

"I told you to go earlier."

Andrew pointed to his gut and grimaced. "Last night's pork . . ."

Fox frowned and unshackled Andrew. "Well, be quick about it. You know where the bathroom is. I shouldn't let you out of my sight, but there's no way I'm following you in there."

"Thanks." Andrew strode the few feet to the back of the swaying train. He locked the bathroom door behind him and bit his lip, trying to contain his excitement. Andrew couldn't suppress a grin. He'd really put one over on Peanut Brain Fox. Still, he hoped there wouldn't be trouble for him. The last thing he wanted was to hurt anyone. Andrew told himself to stay calm but his trembling hands told another story. He was scared. He didn't have much time.

"Breathe," he instructed himself. "Slow and steady wins the race." This well-worn adage of his mother's had served him well in the past but he had never faced anything like this before. Everything, his whole life, was at stake. And the clock was ticking. He didn't have much time.

The train had picked up a bit of steam. It was all right, though. Every hero had to face some danger. Andrew's eyes darted left and right. Sink, toilet, blessed window—his escape route. First he rolled his admission packet up his sleeve, ignoring the warning not to wrinkle, smudge, or deface those precious folders in any way.

Then, catlike, Andrew sprang onto the cold metallic sink. He paused a second. It held his weight. With an acrobatic twist, Andrew reached for the windowsill. Head first he crouched and like a trapeze artist he'd once seen at the circus, catapulted out the window.

It was that easy.

Andrew flew angel-like through the air, arms extended. The roar of the wind in his ears was exhilarating. The fall was something else. There wasn't much to soften his landing besides a clump of crab grass amid the gravel. His right shoulder took the brunt, but the side of his head got banged pretty good too.

There was pain but Andrew didn't mind. From his experience, pain came and went. Physical hurts didn't last as long as the other.

Blood trickled down his cheek into his mouth. The taste was salty sweet, like life itself. Bleeding also eventually stopped, it always had in the past. He lay curled in a ball, fetus-like, his back to the receding train, a hissing behemoth, steaming and heaving away.

What if they saw him now—his teachers, his mother, his father? Would they think him brave and a hero? Or only incorrigible? A worthless truant?

The town of Scranton was gone, far away, and Andrew had no idea where he was. Even the train whistle was now only a memory. All he heard was birdsong and the rustle of leaves in the trees. The countryside, the blessed quiet countryside, where no one knew his name or his story. Where he could rewrite history. His story.

With great effort, Andrew managed to pull the admission packet from his sleeve and breathing heavily, lay back on the damp ground. He wiped some blood from his forehead and using his finger, mixed it with the murky water from a ditch as careful as he'd seen the pharmacist on Maple Street concoct his mother's medicine.

Once the paste was thick enough he rubbed the oozy mixture over the word INCORRIGIBLE. Andrew rubbed and rubbed until the word was blotted out totally.

Then he fished a pencil stub out of his pocket and used it to print in crude blocked letters: ANDREW CHUCK IS A GOOD BOY. The effort exhausted him and he collapsed back toward earth, leaving the evidence to lie next to him by the tracks for someone, anyone, to find.

✝

Karma Recovery
Richard Rosinski

F ran and I were off on another cruise with our friends Ed and Carol. After the ship left the pier, the captain did a 360-degree turn in New York Harbor so everyone could see the Statue of Liberty and the city skyline. Almost everyone headed up to the top decks and crowded around the railing, trying to get a snapshot of the city with their little cameras. At the railing, there was a remarkable couple. The wind was playfully blowing her auburn hair, and he had his arm around her. She was an exact replica of Rita Hayworth in that famous pin-up photo. She was gorgeous. Her companion was the spitting image of Sean Connery in the early James Bond movies. He was gorgeous too. In my own mind I called them Rita and Sean, and told Fran about them.

I don't think I'm unique in this. There are pieces of art that I literally can't get enough of. It's that way with art by Klimt. If I ever saw his painting of Adele Bloch-Bauer in a museum, I think I would just sit and stare for hours. At dinner, I saw Rita and Sean across the room and just watched them, staring at them as if they were paintings in a museum. Fran kicked me and said I was being rude for not paying attention to people at our table. So I turned away and joined our table conversation.

Something started happening and I didn't know if it was real, or just a psychological illusion. I started to see them everywhere I went on the ship. Now this is a small ship, maybe a couple of thousand people. Maybe I just noticed Rita more than any of the others. In the mornings I'd always go to Cafe al Bacio on Deck 5. I'd take my Kindle and try to sit near a window with a cappuccino. I looked up and saw Rita across the room staring at me. When I noticed her, she gave me this big warm smile. Her face lit up as if seeing me was the best, happiest thing that had happened to her all morning. Unused to this kind of reaction, I got flustered and turned to stare out the window.

In the afternoon the four of us were having lunch on the rear deck. Sean walked by, nodded to me, and said, "Hi."

Carol asked, "Do you know him? He acted like he knew you."

"No, not really. Not at all, actually," I said. I don't know why, but I started to feel awkward when running into them.

Before dinner we'd always go to one of our favorite bars. Ed and I worked together for years and both of us left under the same voluntary RIF program. I asked Ed, if he had a chance to start over again, would he do it? Ed said, "Absolutely not. Being retired is the best thing in the world. Do what you want, when you want, with no money or job worries."

I didn't know what I would do. I was very naive through most of my life. I thought that any major problem could be surmounted if I just worked harder. It wasn't until I was in my mid-fifties that I realized how stupid that was. My career didn't really pick up until I realized that the solution to an insurmountable problem is to move, leave, change jobs. I've sometimes wondered how life would have turned out if I figured that out thirty years earlier.

"Haven't you learned that none of it made a difference?" Ed said. "Everything was wired. When you didn't get a promotion and raise, it wasn't because of your work. They were meant for someone else, not you. Working for a big company is like riding on a bus. You can change your seat, but it doesn't matter; it's going to the same place."

"But I got promoted and made a lot of money after I left." I said.

"All you did was change buses." Ed said. He's a cynic.

The first port stop was Boston. We'd been to Boston many times and had no interest in any tourist things. We walked around the Boston Public Gardens, and then went shopping on Newberry Street, a tony district where many of the stores are in converted brownstone buildings. Nearby, Ed found a well-reviewed restaurant. The place was noisy and jammed. We had a long wait. As the waitress was bringing our food over to the table, another couple walked in. I looked over. It was Rita and Sean. I whispered to Fran, "See, I'm not stalking them and it's not just coincidence. Something else is going on."

On every cruise, we make a point of having lunch in the main dining room. The service and selection aren't as good as in the cafeteria, but the waiters assign people randomly at big tables. It's amazing, but strangers will tell you their life story at the slightest provocation. We'd met a man who took this two-week cruise because it coincided with the interval between his chemo treatments. Once a woman told us how her seventy-seven-year-old husband fell off their roof and died on the way to the hospital. Another time we met a woman who had been on this ship for her honeymoon, now she was celebrating her divorce. We meet people we'd never meet otherwise. All the tables were filled, so the waiter started a new one for us. A couple walked up and said, "Do you mind if we join you?" I said, "No, please do."

I looked up and saw it was Rita and Sean. Fran nudged my knee under the table. I said, "My name is Richard and this is Fran."

Sean said, "My name is Richard and this is Fran, too."

"How unusual," I said.

"Not at all," Sean said. "Richard and Frances are very common names. I wouldn't be surprised if there were fifty other Richards and fifty other Frans on the ship. I'll bet some others are paired up. It's like with the lottery. People think that winning the lottery is rare because the odds are two hundred fifty million to one. But somebody wins almost every week. It's improbable, but not rare. Do you bet on the lottery?"

"Occasionally," I said, "only if the prize is five hundred million dollars or more. Then it's a fair bet."

"Good answer. What you are saying is that the prizes aren't the right ones to interest you. Let me ask you, have you ever experienced a life-changing event? Have you ever made a decision that was wrong and you wish you could undo?"

"Yes, my life-changing event was marrying Fran. Without her, I never would have gone to grad school and become a scientist. Without her, I would have been a high school English teacher. One bad decision was that I accepted a job transfer when I didn't know I could refuse it."

"See, now those are prizes that are worth something to you. What if there was a lottery in which the third prize was being able to undo a bad decision, second prize was to have a life-changing event, and first prize was to being able to go back in time and rewrite your own history knowing everything you know now? Would that be a lottery that would interest you?"

"Yes, of course. I'm sure everyone dreams of getting a do-over, but it's impossible, so it's not worth thinking about."

"Well, if that lottery would interest you, prove it. Give me a dollar."

I pulled out my money clip and gave him a dollar bill.

"A man of conviction. You'll find out if you won by the end of the cruise."

I thought that he had just flimflammed me out of a dollar. But it was worth it for some interesting conversation.

We actually saw Rita and Sean often after that. They would join Ed and Carol and Fran and me every day before dinner. They were good company and after a few drinks we had interesting conversations about politics, history, and religion. Rita said that Kissinger was the best diplomat who had ever lived. Sean said that all religions were the same, just seen through different viewpoints. If we saw each other in the cafeteria at breakfast, we'd join them. They were fun to talk to, and I sometimes felt that I was back in a grad school seminar with other smart people. I had breakfast with Rita one morning and I asked her how long she and Sean had been together.

"What do you mean together? Oh, I know, you mean in a relationship. We're not in a relationship or married or anything. We're just on assignment together. We're part of a larger team. In a few months we'll each get different assignments. Right now we work together."

"On an assignment? What do you do?"

"It's related to that comment about different religions. I'm very bad at explaining this. I'm good at doing, but bad at explaining. You should ask him. He understands it all."

Later that day, I bought Sean a double bourbon Manhattan before I asked him to explain the assignment.

"Do you know what Karma is? It's badly understood as 'You get what's coming to you,' or 'You get what you deserve,' that the universe keeps track and punishes bad people. In reality, Karma is the engine behind all religion. But often Karma was misused as an excuse. In India, people are Untouchables because of their bad Karma. Poor people are poor because of bad Karma. It's misallocated. Once a little boy accidentally hit a girl with a baseball bat. His family was assigned two generations of bad Karma. That was clearly a mistake. So, a while ago, it was decided to handle Karma at a local level. The North American district instituted Karma Recovery Teams to make sure that people's lives turn out the way they were supposed to. The prospectors search for Karma errors. Bob and Marge Mitchell in your church are prospectors. They send us a report. We are verifiers. We write a report and send it to headquarters. I'm sure it sounds strange to you, but it's a living. It pays the bills."

What do you do when you meet a crazy person? One minute I'm with this gorgeous couple and the next I feel like Wallace Shawn in the film *My Dinner with Andre*. Andre revealed himself, little by little, to be completely and totally bonkers. I didn't respond or say anything. I just nodded my head. I changed the subject.

I decided I would ignore this derangement. Rita and Sean were marvelous company. Ed and Carol and Fran and I had known each other for over twenty-five years. Yet, Rita and Sean fit right in. They made the cruise more enjoyable. They were fun to be with. They listened to our stories. Rita had traveled to many of the same places that we had. We compared notes on London and Barcelona and Toronto. Besides, the cruise would only last another few days.

We were looking forward to Quebec City. We had all been there before, but this time we would find new sights and restaurants. We were really surprised when, at dinner, Rita and Sean said they would be leaving the ship in Quebec. They were done with this assignment, and today got an email that directed them to meet their next assignment at noon tomorrow in the

Frontenac Hotel. They needed to pack, so this would be our good-bye. I shook Sean's hand and kissed Rita on the cheek. I felt sad and disappointed.

After Quebec, on the next night of the cruise, I stayed up too late and had too much to drink. In the morning, a little sliver of light came in at the edge of the curtains. I felt really strange, but in a good way. I had slept through the night without waking to go to the bathroom. My hips and knees didn't ache for the first time in months, years maybe. But I had a little hangover. *Was there a party?* I looked across the bed and saw a thin, young woman who was beautiful, gorgeous even. She looked vaguely familiar. *What the heck did I do last night?* I turned on the light and went into the bathroom. I looked in the mirror. I moved from side to side. I waved my hands at the mirror. Very strange. The image in the mirror was me, but not the current me. It was the me that could only be seen in thirty-year-old photographs.

Suddenly I understood. I ran back into the room and yelled, "Fran, wake up. Sean and Rita erased our Karma. We get to do our lives all over again!"

Fran looked at herself in the mirror on the wall. "What should we tell Ed and Carol?"

"If we are thirty years younger, we haven't met them yet."

✝

Library Time
Laurel Bruce

An ear-splitting clap of thunder rumbled ominously as Susie searched the library computer. Her friend, Laura, kept a wary eye on the windows in the children's room of the public library.

"Hurry up, Susie! It's going to start raining any minute!"

"I need to find this one book. Miss Lawrence recommended it."

"Well, then, ask Miss Lawrence to help you find it," Laura said.

"I would, except Miss Lawrence is helping those girls over there."

Susie indicated a row of books where Miss Lawrence stood with three girls. Miss Lawrence was the children's librarian for as long as Susie could remember. Some kids said she was so old she was around when their parents were kids! Susie admired Miss Lawrence. She was pretty, even if her short hair had turned gray.

Lightning flashed and another clap of thunder rumbled through the sky.

"Susie!"

"Chill out, Laura!" Susie admonished. "It's just a little old storm."

The lights flickered. Everything went dark.

The lights came back on instantly.

"Thank goodness!" Laura said.

Susie returned to searching on the computer. But there was no computer to search on. "The computers are missing!"

The row of computers Susie and Laura had been using were replaced with a row of tiny drawers. A boy about their age thumbed through some cards in one of the drawers. He glanced at Susie.

"Hey, kid!" the boy said. "You spazzin'? You gotta be quiet in the library."

"Sorry," Susie mumbled. She reached for the library books she had selected. But they were missing too.

"Where are my books?" Susie said. "I put them right here!"

"Shh!" Another kid shot daggers at Susie.

"Sorry," Susie said. She turned to find Laura staring wide-eyed at the children's room.

"Everything is so . . . orange," Laura said.

The two middle-school-aged girls faced a children's room that was not the bright, spacious room they knew. The blue plastic tables with all the colorful chairs—red, green, yellow, blue—were replaced with dark wood tables and orange vinyl chairs. Even the librarian's desk and the bookshelves matched the dark wood of the tables.

A little girl, about five years old, approached the librarian's desk. She hugged a rag doll.

"Hello, Charity," a gorgeous blond-haired woman said. "I see you brought Miss Dolly to story hour today."

"Yes, Miss Lawrence," the little girl said. "She likes to hear the story, too."

Susie's and Laura's eyes bugged out at the librarian.

Miss Lawrence had been transformed! Could this lady who looked like she was in her early twenties be the same Miss Lawrence they knew?

"Charity, please don't run off from Daddy like that!"

An absolutely dreamy guy rushed into the children's room. His auburn hair matched that of his daughter's.

"I'm sorry, Daddy. But this is Miss Lawrence."

Charity looked expectantly from Miss Lawrence to her father. Susie grinned. Was Charity trying to hook her dad up?

"Miss Lawrence!" Charity's father said. "I'm Chance McKay. My daughter adores you. Last night I was reading a story to Charity and she told me, 'You don't tell it good like Miss Lawrence.'"

Miss Lawrence blushed. "Oh, I'm sure you tell stories very well, Mr. McKay."

"Miss Lawrence, I'm having a small party at my house on Tuesday. I was wondering if would like to—"

"Chance! Darling! There you are!"

Everyone in the children's room gaped as a stunning raven-haired woman bedecked in jewels and wearing shorts and a tank top breezed into the room.

Some kids snickered. But Susie, Laura, and everyone else in the room watched in rapt attention as the woman grabbed Chance McKay's wrist.

"Melinda! What are you doing here?"

Melinda pouted. "You've forgotten! You invited me. Then you and I and sweet little Charity here are going to a picnic at my parents' home."

Melinda smiled at Miss Lawrence. "What a wonderfully quaint little building. When was it built? In the 1700s?"

"1896," Miss Lawrence said.

"Chance is always telling me what a lovely little town Pequot City is. I could get used to living here."

"Melinda, dear, why don't we go over to the story area and find a seat?"

Chance McKay escorted Melinda and Charity toward the back of the room. Miss Lawrence picked up several picture books and followed them.

Susie was not sure what happened to Charity's mother. But the little girl looked most unhappy with Melinda showing attention to her father. And that's when Susie had the most diabolical idea. She stuck her left foot out as Melinda passed.

Melinda stumbled and collided with Miss Lawrence. She yanked Miss Lawrence's arm to keep from falling. Picture books flew as the two women tumbled to the floor with an awful thud. Melinda and Miss Lawrence tussled on the floor. Melinda grabbed Miss Lawrence's hair. But Miss Lawrence stopped moving and went limp.

"FIGHT!"

Kids crowded around the two women as Chance tried to break up the fracas. He managed to pull Melinda up as another librarian ran into the room.

"Break it up!" the librarian shouted.

Miss Lawrence lay unmoving under a pile of picture books.

"Susie!" Laura said. "Miss Lawrence is dead—and it's your fault!"

"It was an accident. I meant to hurt Melinda."

"It's a cinch we can't stay here," Laura said. She dragged Susie toward the library entrance. "We have to go. I told Logan we'd meet him at the Ice Cream Bar."

Susie and Laura left the library and raced toward Main Street to meet Laura's brother.

The two girls reached Main Street and searched for the Ice Cream Bar.

"It's not here!" Laura said.

"It has to be," Susie said. "This *is* Main Street."

The two girls ran along Main Street. But it was not the Main Street they knew. A movie theater stood where the Ice Cream Bar was supposed to be. People were lining up to see something called *The Empire Strikes Back*.

A department store stood at the other end of Main Street.

"What's Orr's?" Susie asked.

"It's a store from the olden days," Laura said. "My mother said she shopped in this store when she was a little girl."

"How come I never heard of it?"

"It closed, Susie." Laura's eyes grew wide. "It closed a long time ago."

A shiver ran down Susie's spine. "This is where the toy store is supposed to be. I'm sure of it."

"You're right," Laura said. "We're not going to find Logan are we?"

"No. Not in whatever year we are in."

Laura whined. "What are we going to do?"

"We're going back to the library," Susie said. "Maybe we can figure out what year this is. Plus if I killed Miss Lawrence, then I have to face the consequences."

The two girls stepped onto the street as an ancient vehicle bore down on them. The vehicle honked at them, and the girls jumped out of the way.

"What was that?" Laura asked.

"I think it was a car."

"Yeah? What were those things on the front of it? They looked like owl's eyes!"

By the time Susie and Laura returned to Church Street, thunder again rumbled across the sky and it rained. The girls dashed into the library and raced into the children's room.

"The computers are back!" Susie said.

"And all the furniture is like it's supposed to be!" Laura said.

"And there are the library books I picked out!"

Susie raced over to the books like they were old friends. She and Laura hugged each other.

"We're home!"

"Well, Susie and Laura, how can I help you?"

A pretty librarian with short, gray hair approached them. The two girls were astounded.

"Miss Lawrence!" Laura said. "You're not dead!"

"I beg your pardon." The librarian turned pale.

Susie glared at Laura. "She means you look so beautiful."

"Thank you," Miss Lawrence said. "But the name Lawrence. That was my maiden name. How did you know that?"

"How did we—?"

"I've been Mrs. McKay for longer than the two of you have been alive."

Susie and Laura grinned.

"The little girl—Charity," Susie said. "You married her dad!"

"Charity is my stepdaughter. How do you know her?"

"We met her here at the library," Susie said.

"Yeah," Laura said.

But neither girl told Mrs. McKay *when* they met her.

✝

Memory Lane Ain't What It Used to Be
Phil Giunta

A midsummer stroll down Memory Lane turned out to be far less nostalgic than Gene and Dottie Spencer had anticipated. In fact, it was downright depressing.

"Did we make a wrong turn?" Dottie glanced from one end of the street to the other. "Where's old Burt Hepworth's Dutch colonial . . . and the Marconi's bungalow?" Gene pointed to a row of modern, nondescript townhouses incongruously crammed between two Cape Cods. "Oh." Dottie frowned. "Well, I guess everything changes."

"And not for the better." Gene shook his head at the glut of vehicles parked bumper-to-bumper along both sides of the narrow street. "It was never like this in our day. There must be four cars to every house . . . and we wouldn't dream of letting our sidewalks go to pot like this, all cracked and buckling with weeds everywhere. Don't people take pride in their neighborhood anymore?"

For the Spencers, Memory Lane took the form of Sandalwood Drive near the outskirts of the city. It was here that the couple had purchased their first and only home nearly sixty years ago. It was here that they had raised three children, made lifelong friends, and become pillars of the community. Now, however, all of that was ancient history and one that had obviously lost much of its luster.

"I'm almost afraid to see what our old house looks like now," Gene grumbled. "Remember what Carmen said to Gayle and Alex the other day while we were watching over the grandkids? The new owner is some single gal—"

"Single *young lady*," Dottie corrected.

75

"—that Carmen used to work with. She gave the place a makeover before moving in, so expect to see some changes."

Finally, they stopped at the corner of Sandalwood and Highland Avenue and peered up at the rustic two-story colonial.

Gene threw up his hands. "Now why did she replace a perfectly good metal roof with shingles? Remember when my brother and I used to get up there every summer and paint it?"

"And every summer you griped about the heat."

Gene leaned forward and peered over the neatly trimmed boxwoods along the front of the house. "And she replaced the old wooden porch with concrete. Remember how I used to varnish it to a perfect sheen every spring?"

"And every spring you bellyached about your hay fever."

"Those were the days. Hey, remember—"

The roar of a lawnmower engine curtailed any further reminiscing. Gene and Dottie followed the noise around the corner, stopping at a chain link fence that enclosed the backyard. There, a slim young woman in a sweat-soaked tank top and denim shorts pushed the mower across a narrow lawn speckled with dandelions and white clover.

Gene folded his arms. "You know, back in our day, single young ladies didn't own homes or mow lawns."

"The world's a different place now, Gene. Like I said earlier, everything changes. Oh, damn!" Dottie pointed toward the shed in the back corner of the yard. "That hussy tore out my blue hydrangeas . . . and our dogwood tree. I used to love to watch it bloom pink every spring."

"Like you said, everything changes. At least she kept the red maple in the middle of the yard. Remember when you and I planted that about five years after we moved in? Now it's taller than the house."

"Speaking of which, I wonder how it looks inside."

"If what we've seen so far is any indication, we probably wouldn't recognize the place."

Dottie put her hand on Gene's chest. "Look, the cellar doors are open. Let's sneak in for a quick look."

"I don't think that's a good idea, Dottie. We should be getting home."

"What's the hurry? We have all the time in the world. We'll be in and out before she finishes cutting the grass." Dottie dashed through the gate and across the yard.

"Dottie, wait! Oh, good grief." Gene followed, but didn't speak again until they had descended through the doors and were standing in the basement. "What's gotten into you?"

"It's like being young again. Off on another escapade!" Dottie beamed. "Like the old days when we were dating. Remember?"

"Of course I remember. Ghost hunting on Halloween night in the cemetery across from your parents' house, skinny dipping in the lake up the road from the high school."

"Climbing out on the roof of your uncle's beach house in the middle of the night to stargaze."

Gene grinned. "The heavens weren't the only thing we admired that night."

"Hence the reason we named our first born after your uncle."

"Yeah, I guess two old souls like us deserve one last adventure," Gene motioned Dottie ahead, "but let's make it quick. I feel like we're intruding. At least the steps are still in the same place, and just as solid as the day I built them."

"You always did good work, love." Dottie reached the top of the stairs first. For a moment, she froze in the doorway before turning back to her husband. "Brace yourself, Gene."

"Why?"

Dottie stepped aside as they emerged into the dining room.

"It's gone!" Gene cried. "All the blue and green floral wallpaper I put up for you. It's all gone." Instead, the walls throughout the entire first floor were painted a conservative antique white. His shoulders slumped. "It's like our past has been swept away. Our home has lost all of its character."

"It's not our home anymore, Gene," Dottie reminded him. "We changed the décor when we moved in. Why can't the new owner do the same?"

"But it's as if . . ." Gene's voice quivered as he leaned against the wall and lowered his head.

". . . we were never here at all," Dottie finished. She gripped her husband's shoulders and gently maneuvered him away from the wall. "Come on, Gene. Let's go upstairs."

"What's the point?"

"Humor me, Gene. We'll never come back here again after today, I promise."

⸺

It was more of the same on the second floor. Every inch of wallpaper had been removed and the hallway painted with the same drab off-white as the first floor. The three bedrooms were a different matter. Each had been given its own distinct color.

"Well, that's something at least." Gene entered the smallest of them, once Alex's room, which the new owner had converted into a home office. He ran a gentle finger down the wall alongside the door trim just as Dottie joined him.

"Remember how we used to measure the kids' heights on the wall here every year and mark them in pencil?" Gene said. "That's all gone now."

"I know." Dottie moved past Gene toward the opposite wall where a series of color images printed on letter-sized paper were pinned to a corkboard. "Oh, Gene, these are pictures of the house from years ago." She pointed to each one in turn as she continued. "That's you and I sitting on the porch the way it used to look . . . and there's you and Alex up on the roof getting ready to paint it . . . and Carmen and Gayle standing with their prom dates under the pink dogwood. You can see the blue hydrangeas and . . ." Dottie's voice cracked as she covered her mouth and leaned against her husband. "This was our life, Gene. Where did she get these?"

Gene kissed away the tears from her cheek and glanced down at the desk. "Apparently, from this." He held up a 4x6 photo album and began flipping through it before handing it to Dottie.

"And here's a letter addressed to our daughter." Gene picked up the paper from atop the laser printer and stepped over to the window. "Dear Carmen, I found this little photo album in the attic and wanted to return it to you. I hope you don't mind that I made color copies of some of the photos as a way of preserving the beautiful work your parents put into the property. As you know, the metal roof had rusted and some planks on the old porch had rotted since your parents lived here. The dogwood tree succumbed to some kind of disease and had to be removed, but I am doing my best to maintain as much as of the old charm as possible while also making it low maintenance for me—"

"See? Told you, Gene. She's just making the house her own. Our past hasn't been entirely swept away. Despite all that's changed in the old neighborhood, someone here will still remember us."

Gene set the letter on the desk. "You're right, Dottie—as always." He tilted his head. "Hey, the lawnmower stopped. We'd better go."

Dottie laid the photo album atop the letter and followed her husband downstairs. They dashed across the living room until Gene halted abruptly at the front door.

Dottie nearly collided with him. "Now what?"

"A gray steel door? She had to replace this, too? Remember that beautiful mahogany and glass door I hung all by myse—"

"Gene!"

"Just saying." He stepped aside and motioned for Dottie to precede him. "Ladies first."

She rolled her eyes and hurried out to the porch. "I can't blame her for putting in a steel door. She's a single young woman and this isn't like the old days."

"So you keep reminding me!"

Rewriting the Past

"Well, at least the old firehouse is still where it used to be," Gene said as they crossed the final street on their journey. "So many fond memories of volunteering with those crazy guys."

"And I was delighted to see St. Margaret's soup kitchen is still serving the poor," Dottie added. "I always enjoyed cooking for them after the kids were out on their own."

"I know you did, Dottie. You were always God's little helper."

Eventually, they came upon the familiar green wrought iron fence of home. Dottie sighed. "Be it ever so humble."

"Well, at least we know most of the people here, and it doesn't change very much."

"Except when new neighbors arrive." Dottie hooked her arm through Gene's as they passed beyond the front gate of Holy Cross Cemetery and vanished beneath a canopy of swaying pink dogwoods and red maples.

Monologue
John Evans

G ranville Roberts entered his bedroom but did not turn on the
light. Instead, he worked his way over to the window and opened
the curtains to a flood of moonlight. It washed over his bed, a wingback
chair, and his desk. He had moved his desk to the bedroom for those awful
nights when he could not sleep and could roll out of bed and do some work.
But the desk was not cluttered with any evidence of work. It was starkly
equipped with a leather desk pad, a pen in a brass holder, and a picture
frame.

The frame contained a photograph of his wife, Eleanor, from an earlier
time, before their marriage. In the ghostly glow of moonlight, Granville
could barely see her timeless beauty and enigmatic expression. He didn't
need the light—the features were burned into his memory. Her lips, slightly
parted, seemed ready to burst into a smile of pleasure—or a grimace of
disapproval. The eyes, narrowed, sparkled with the promise of tears of joy—
or anguish. The tilt of her head expressed both interest and doubt. In the
months after her death, Granville talked to the picture as if Eleanor were
still alive and sitting across from him at the kitchen table. As time passed,
the picture seemed to communicate with him, giving him counsel in all
matters. He tapped into her wellspring of emotions and withdrew the exact
response he sought from her. He found it comforting.

Granville lowered himself into the chair at the desk. He pulled open the
right-hand drawer and peered in, knowing it would be empty, but he had to
check. He hitched forward, leaning in toward the picture and folded his
hands prayerfully and took a deep breath.

"I think she's coming back tonight . . . and I'm scared. I've never seen her so angry."

He turned toward the window and looked out over the silvery lawn and driveway curving through shrubs that looked like black sheep grazing in the moonlight.

"I think it was the first time I've said no to her. Maybe we were wrong to be so . . ." He paused, searching for the right word—agreeable, generous, lenient, permissive. "I think we've spoiled her," he said finally, turning back toward the picture. The tilt of Eleanor's head demanded an explanation.

"I don't know why I said no. When I was in college, vacation time meant returning to the mill—I couldn't afford *not* to work. When Beth told me she was going to Barcelona on spring break, I resented it. She didn't ask —she *told* me she was going, like it was her divine right to do whatever she wanted. I put my foot down—I said, 'No!' and something snapped. Her eyes blazed and she stormed up to her room. The house shook when she slammed the door. Later that night, she left. I didn't hear her go. But the BMW was gone in the morning, and my gun is missing—and I'm afraid of what she might do."

Granville rose and paced behind his desk stealing a glance or two at the picture. Eleanor seemed even more doubtful. He stopped and locked eyes with the picture, determined to be firm.

"This is not easy for me to tell you. I'm embarrassed by what's been going through my head in the last few days, but I've got to be honest. When we first met . . . when we were falling in love, I had my doubts. You were young and beautiful and wealthy. I was old and average and poor. You also had a daughter. I did the math, looking into the future. I would be in my seventies by the time Beth was in college and I didn't know if I was ready for that. What I didn't see in the future was the fact that you wouldn't be with me—that I would be alone, raising a young girl . . . and here I am."

Granville slid back into his seat and looked away for a moment. "The funny thing is," he said with a wry smile, "I've loved every minute of it— until you went away." He folded his hands and stared at the picture for a moment before continuing. "And Beth—I fell in love with her the first time we met, but she never loved me. Not to the degree that I loved her. I could feel it. She tolerated me. And now . . ." He lowered his head. "I'm not sure she even does that."

He turned to the window. The wind had picked up and whistled mournfully through the bare branches. He returned his attention to the picture and studied Eleanor's expression, but it told him nothing. The face seemed strangely blank as if weighing his words and waiting patiently for more. Granville was still for a long time before speaking.

"I've been pouring over this for days, and I feel so guilty about what I'm thinking, but here goes—it's all about money. We never talked money—never had to. We had everything we'd ever wanted . . . always, and so has Beth. Every birthday wish fulfilled. Every item on her Christmas list was always neatly wrapped under the tree. And special gifts for special occasions —the BMW for graduation.

"It's the Me Generation. Instant gratification. Me! Me! Me! I want it now! No pride in working for something. No understanding of how longing for something makes it sweeter. It has to be NOW.

"I tried looking at it from Beth's perspective . . . and I didn't like what I saw. Let's follow the money. You married into money, and Beth, she was born into it. Richard died and the money became yours. Then I married you —married into money. And when you left, the money became mine. Beth went from having a wealthy mother to having an old stepfather in control of her future. If I were to marry and die, she could lose everything. The blood ties are gone. The family bond no longer exists. She's a young adult with a total stranger in charge of what should be her inheritance. There's only way to break that chain of events, only one thing to do."

Granville rose and shuffled to the window. He spread his hands on the deep sill with his nose inches from the pane—each breath marked by a throbbing burst of fog on the glass. For many minutes he remained still, staring at nothing while convincing himself that he was about to do the right thing. And when he was certain that he was right, he went over his plan detail by detail, searching for a weakness, a flaw. But there were so many variables, so many possibilities.

His mind drifted off to the distant past—to a time when he first met

Beth. She was a toddler then and Eleanor asked him to watch over her while she met with Marcus Freeman, her lawyer. "Watch her like a mother!" she smiled.

There was a park across the street with pathways, picnic tables, and a playground. Beth was attracted to the jungle gym and tried the swings and the slide, and crossed the rope bridge that led to the monkey bars, giggling with every step. Granville hoisted her up so she could grab the bar and stepped back with Beth hanging from the second rung by little hands too weak for her weight. She fell.

Granville lunged forward and caught her under the arms and swung her up into the air like it was part of the fun. Beth laughed, unaware of the danger she had passed through.

Granville did not share that moment with Eleanor. He savored it as something special. He had watched Beth "like a woman" and found that protecting such innocence from pain and misfortune was the greatest feeling in the world, and he wanted to be Beth's guardian angel forever.

If only he could do it one more time.

Granville tensed when the BMW slid through the moonlight, headlamps off, at a cautious speed, winding its way noiselessly to the house. He stood erect at parade rest with his hands clasped behind his back and watched as it neared and finally disappeared from his line of sight. He remained still, eyes closed, as his mind traced Beth's progress to the rear driveway, through the garage to the kitchen, and up the wide staircase. He could visualize her stopping on the landing to listen and steel herself before continuing to the top. A few silent strides and she would be at his door.

There was a faint click and the pressure in the room seemed to change. Granville did not move. He felt her presence, and pictured her paralyzed by his silhouette in the moonlit window.

"Hello, Beth," he said without turning. His tone was flat, betraying neither fear nor love. "I thought you might come back tonight." He paused for a second. "I saw your car approaching the house. Headlights not working?" He grunted pleasantly. "That never looks good on security videos."

Granville said nothing else for a moment and turned to face his daughter and pulled the golden chain on the desk lamp. He was quick to notice the shock and confusion that left her frozen and unsure. And he noticed her right hand tucked behind her thigh.

"I had a long talk with your mother just now," he began. "I really miss her. I was about to join her . . ." He paused to emphasize his next words, "But my gun is missing."

Beth took a step toward him, but he held up his hand and she stopped mid-stride.

"Before you say anything—do anything—please, hear me out."

Her muscles relaxed and Granville continued.

"Ever since you came into my life, it has been my greatest pleasure to save you from the pain the world could inflict—and you never knew.

"Remember this Christmas present?" He held up his wrist, displaying the watch that he had worn for the past seven years.

"I overheard you telling your friend Tanya that you were going to steal it from Brixton's Jewelry. Jake Brixton happens to be a friend of mine. I told him you were doing a research paper on shoplifting and wanted first-hand experience. I bought the watch, and he let you steal it. By the way, Jake told me you were the worst thief he had ever encountered."

Granville smiled at the memory, and when the smile faded he continued. "I've been doing that your entire life—saving you from yourself. And here we are again—one last time. I'm afraid you are about to do something that will put you in jail for the rest of your life." He shook his head. "I can't let that happen to you . . . especially if there is a better way—a safer way." He paused for several heartbeats. "Let me do it."

They locked eyes, and Granville tried to read her emotions. He was hoping for remorse, shame—even a glimmer of love or fear. But Beth seemed simply stunned.

"Meanwhile, you are going to need an alibi. Barcelona works—spring break with your friends. You said they are leaving today. You can join them there. It's not too late."

He stepped over to his desk and pulled a manila packet out of the left side drawer. "I've thought about this since our little tiff. I need to make things right." He held the packet out for her inspection. "Here is your passport, plane tickets, hotel reservations at the Crowne Plaza, and a credit card in your name. You can ask for a different room once you get there." His mind drifted off to thoughts of being with Eleanor and he continued in a softer voice. "And, of course, you'll need to arrange for an earlier return flight after . . ." He let the rest of the thought die. "The airlines are very accommodating when it comes to grieving family members."

Granville stood silently for a moment, tapping his palm with the packet.

"Well, there you have it. I shall be off with your mother and you will get what you so richly deserve." His smile was both warm and sad. "Leave the gun," he said, and dropped the packet on the desk with a grunt of humor. "Take the cannoli. This is an offer you can't refuse."

Granville turned and struck his parade rest pose at the window. The matter was now closed. He held that position until the BMW sped down the driveway, lights on. Then he turned and stared at his .357 sitting in the pool of light on his desk. He smiled. His eyes shifted over to the picture of Eleanor, and his smile broadened. "That went better than I thought."

He stepped over to the wingback chair, flopped into it and stared at the moon until he fell asleep.

The morning sun was high in the sky when he awoke. His first thought was of Beth, and he grabbed his iPhone to locate her using a family mapping application. Its accuracy was spotty with air travel, but it showed that Beth was still over the water and nearing Europe. He punched in a number and waited until a male voice answered.

"Marcus? The bird has left the nest," was all he said and pocketed his phone.

Granville pulled a large suitcase from beneath the bed skirt and opened it on the comforter. He picked up the picture of Eleanor from his desk and said, "Good morning, Dear. I want to apologize for last night. I know it was unpleasant, but it needed to be done—and I have a surprise for you. We are checking off one more item on our bucket list. We are going to Paris for a year. I rented an apartment on the Left Bank, where I shall paint. Marcus will handle our affairs here. He will also cancel Beth's hotel reservation, return flight, her credit card, and iPhone account. Marcus will handle her college costs for her senior year and any emergencies that arise. He will decide what constitutes an emergency. Our only contact with her will be through Marcus. She must fend for herself. Beth is now officially enrolled in the School of Hard Knocks and classes start today."

Granville delicately placed the picture in the suitcase and studied the face. There was a smile of approval about to burst forth, and he gave her a wink. "It's going to be all right."

And he closed the lid and snapped the latches.

✝

An Outside Chance
Bart Palamaro

The comfortable, companionable atmosphere of the First Class Smoking Room perfectly suits the wealthy men taking their ease late in the fourth evening of the voyage. The murmur of quiet conversation, the *slip-slap* of cards on the baize table covers, the occasional exclamation as someone makes a particularly good play. Fine cigar smoke fills the air along with the clink-splash of vintage brandies being poured.

Lord Peter watches a game of poker between several Americans and an English peer, when a low grumbling sound interrupts his amused contemplation. He looks around as some of the other occupants glance up at the annoying distraction, then return to their cards when the sound stops.

He wanders over to the bar.

The barman, alert even though the hour is growing toward midnight, asks, "Another brandy, my lord?"

"No, thank you, Parker," replies Lord Peter. "Er, Parker, did you hear that odd sound just now?"

"Yes, my lord."

"D'ye know what it was?"

"No, my lord." He thinks for a moment, "I don't believe I've ever heard anything like it before."

Lord Peter cocks his head, listens. Something in the ship's atmosphere is missing. "Have the engines gone off?"

"I believe they may have, my lord."

"Oh, 'at'll be a thrown prop, I expect." Collins, the other barman, walks around the bar carrying a tray filled with empty glasses. Even twenty years at sea hasn't dimmed his East End Irish accent. "I 'eard just the same on the old *Star o' India*. Back in '93 it was, me lord. Just off Sout'ampton, from Lisbon, we was, after goin' round Cape 'orn. Lucky fer us we was in sight o' the point. No Marconi back then. They 'ad to tow the ol' girl in." Collins chuckles at the recollection as he puts the glasses in the washbasin under the bar.

Lord Peter quietly reflects on the relaxation of social class engendered by late hours, comfortable surroundings, and a ship's intimate company. None of his father's staff, or his own valet for that matter, would even think of speaking to him as casually as Collins had. At age twenty, Lord Peter is still too young to realize that he himself has put these men at ease over the last four days by his respect for them. Never would they presume on the acquaintance, but at this hour, with this man, and under these circumstances they feel relaxed enough to speak as they might to a senior shipmate.

"I heard Mr. Ismay's been pushing the captain to get as much speed out of her as he can," offers Parker. He shakes his head. "Owners meddling in the running of the ship, it can't be good, my lord."

"True, me lord," Collins adds. "They say Captain Smith 'as been pushin' 'ard to beat the old crossin' record, over twenty-two knots we been going. I don't think I've ever 'eard engines sound like the last few hours. Likely we've just thrown a prop." Collins sounds glum at the thought. "There goes our crossin' record, an' the Blue Riband."

"Mmmm . . . you may be right, Collins. Still . . ." Lord Peter trails off as a faraway look comes into his eyes. "It can't hurt . . ."

Collins and Parker slip each other a smile. Long-time shipmates, they can communicate with a raised eyebrow, a glance, or sometimes, it seems, mental telepathy. They genuinely like Lord Peter and are amused by his sometimes whimsical manner. But, shrewd judges of character that they are, they know the whimsy hides a startlingly sharp intelligence.

Lord Peter suddenly straightens and stares past the two barmen with unseeing eyes. "Good God!" He turns and hurries from the First Class Smoking Room without saying another word.

Leaving Collins and Parker communicating silently behind him, Lord Peter quickly makes his way to the A Deck forward railing. On the deck below him, in the clear, bright starlight, several men and women in evening clothes are having a bit of a frolic kicking large chunks of something around. He feels his face go white as he realized what it is. Ice! He races to the starboard rail and peers back along the great ship's wake. There! Is that a flicker of white? Just below where the horizon meets the dark water? In the still, star-filled night it is hard to be sure, but . . . "Let's see," Lord Peter calculates quickly, "at twenty-two knots we'd be going, umm, a bit over a third of a mile (a *nautical* mile, he remembers) a minute. It's been, what, four or five minutes since that odd sound? So if it was an iceberg we hit, then it would only be a mile and a half or so behind us." He looks again, tries to pick out the spot in the darkness. No use. Have his eyes played tricks? But those chunks of ice on the deck below are no illusion. He looks down again. Some young buck scoops up a bit of ice, drops it in his drink and sips. No, no illusion.

Recalling his visit to the wheelhouse and chart room on the first day of the voyage, Lord Peter moves quickly forward to the stairs. As he takes the steps two at a time the inane memory comes to him that a staircase is called a *ladder* aboard ship. Making his way to the bridge area he pushes into the wheelhouse past a startled seaman.

"Sir!"

A younger man in an officer's uniform steps up. "I'm sorry sir, but no visitors are allowed without—"

"Where's the captain?" interrupts Lord Peter.

"Sir, I must ask you to return to the passenger decks."

"Where is the captain?" The accents of the aristocracy are plain in Lord Peter's voice, a voice that is accustomed to delivering orders and having them obeyed. Nevertheless the young officer persists in his duty. "Sir, please. The captain is extremely busy at the moment and—"

A man in an overcoat thrown over his pajamas and a sheaf of rolled up blueprints shoulders Lord Peter aside and hurries into the chart room, kicking the door shut behind him. It is Thomas Andrews, the representative from the firm of Harland and Wolff who is accompanying the *Titanic* on her maiden voyage. He isn't just any representative, but the engineer in charge of the Harland and Wolff shipyard. He is the man who designed the *Titanic*. That sets the notion Lord Peter has been harboring into a chilling certainty.

With no hesitation Lord Peter simply walks past the stammering young officer and opens the chart room door. Inside, Bruce Ismay, Captain Smith, and two of his senior officers anxiously watch the engineer struggle with his blueprints. At last the plans are unrolled on the chart table.

"She's breached from the bow, Compartment One." Andrews taps the print, "Here. All the way to Six on the starboard side. I measured over twelve feet already in Number Four, Captain." He turns, looks Smith directly in the eye. "There's no way to save her, sir. She's going down."

"What? This ship can't sink!" Ismay practically shouts the words.

The captain turns to Ismay. "Calmly, sir, calmly please." Then he's back to Andrews. "What about the watertight doors, the pumps?"

"The watertight doors have already been closed, sir. But it won't be enough. Those watertight bulkheads only go up to E Deck. With six compartments open to the sea she will be dragged down by the bow as it fills. The water will then spill over into each successive compartment as the bow goes deeper." Andrews replies. "And the pumps. Well, they buy us an hour or so at the most. Within two hours, maybe two and a half, this ship will be on the bottom of the Atlantic."

"Shoring up, can't we shore up the breach?" Captain Smith is now sounding desperate.

Andrews shakes his head, "Sorry, sir. It is already too late for that and there are multiple breaches in all six compartments. The damage is too widespread."

Each man in the room struggles to absorb what this actually means. Ismay and Andrews exchange a shocked glance. The captain and his officers stare at the plans, then at one another. Each of them searches for denial on the others' faces. Each waits for the words someone would say:

"Oh, that won't happen because . . ." or, "No, look here, if we just . . ."

But no words are spoken, and the silence stretches out.

Just inside the chart room door, Lord Peter and the young officer stand paralyzed by the stunning announcement: *Two and a half hours.*

Absorbed by the enormity of the event, none of the others is yet aware of them.

"Sir," Andrews speaks into the heavy silence, "you must order 'Abandon Ship.' The sooner the orders are given the better."

His sentence unlocks a dam.

"Sir, we must alert the deck crew—"

"Sir, a wireless distress message—"

"How dare you suggest—" This last from Ismay.

"Silence!" Captain Smith's order cuts off the babble. "Boxall, alert the crew to prepare for launching lifeboats. Lightoller, wake the stewards and maids. Have them start waking the passengers and prepare them to abandon ship. Andrews, can I call upon your staff to do as much as possible to slow the intake?"

He turns, noticing Lord Peter and the young officer for the first time. "You, Mister ahh . . . Moody. Wake the rest of the officers, inform them what has transpired and ask them to report here for instructions . . ."

"Excuse me, Captain," Lord Peter speaks for the first time. "I believe there—"

Normally deferential to the point of obsequiousness at any hint of aristocracy, Smith interrupts Lord Peter. "I know who you are, my lord, but we are in a serious situation here and time is of the essence. I must ask you to return to your cabin and await instructions. Mister Moody, the rest of you, carry out your orders."

Lord Peter is barely out of Oxford and younger than the junior officer beside him. Normally quiet and courteous, his accent and the weight of upper class power are in full force with his next question. "Do you insist on losing your ship then, sir?"

The entire cabin is suddenly tight with uncertainty. Is this a challenge to the captain's authority? A know-nothing toff with half-baked ideas? Or a genuine chance to save the ship?

It's the latter thought that freezes everyone in place.

Smith's years of experience and authority as captain lend him a solemn air as he eyes the young aristocrat. "You have a suggestion, a solution, young sir? Then by all means let us hear it."

Lord Peter nods his acknowledgment. "My degree, sir, gentlemen, is not engineering or ship design, but history. As such forgive me if I ask some basic questions about our . . . predicament."

"Quickly, my lord. As I said, time is of the essence."

"Yes. As I understand the problem is twofold. One, water is coming in too fast for the pumps to keep up and, two, the holes are too widespread to be effectively blocked from the inside."

Andrews answers, "That, though simplistic, is the essence, yes."

Lord Peter takes a surreptitious breath. "Then why not plug them from the outside, as the old sailors plugged round-shot holes?"

"You are speaking of fothering a sail, but we have no sails."

"No, but you have drapes and rugs and blankets and canvas for all I know."

There is a momentary silence. Boxhall breaks it. "Captain, it may be worth trying. Even if we only slow the ingress, the pumps will give us time. Time to get everyone off. Time for other ships to arrive."

Andrews adds, "*Titanic* is straight sided, no flare, so anything we sink alongside the hull will be close and should be sucked into the damaged areas by water pressure alone. Any heavy fabric should seal these breaches. All we need is a way to—"

Captain Smith cuts through the discussion. "Enough, gentlemen. Mister Andrews redirect your crew to supervise fabrication of some sort of material, and I don't care what it is or what you have to commandeer. Be sure you determine with great care where these 'fothers' should be set. Mister Lightoller, wake the carpenter and have his men assist Mister Andrews. Be sure to include anyone who can sew. There's bound to be some old sail makers among the crew, the bosun will know. Mister Moody . . ."

Minutes later, in the First Class Smoking Room, astonished passengers watch crewmen tear the heavy draperies from the windows, roll them up and drag them out to A Deck. On the Boat Deck, passengers gathering around their assigned lifeboats are treated to the sight of grizzled sailors sitting cross-legged on the deck, sewing grommets into expensive draperies, then attaching weights to one end and one-inch line to the other.

The Number One lifeboat is being lowered, its scratch crew struggles with the awkward burden passed to them over the railing. A man in pajamas, slippers, and an overcoat carefully measures out the length of line as they lower it toward the inky black water.

Behind them, the old sailors are already working on another one.

⌇

Saturday, April 20, at 4:00 p.m., three days later than scheduled, *RMS Titanic* docks in New York. Press accolades praise Captain Smith and his officers for their quick and original thinking and brave actions. It is a crowning finale to a distinguished lifetime of service for the captain, and sure to advance the careers of each and every officer.

A dazzling display of fireboats throwing arcs of water in every direction accompanies a cacophony of ship whistles as the *Titanic* eases into her berth. Press and dignitaries crowd the wharf, eager to honor the crew, grab some reflected glory, and gather stories from the passengers. The original rag-tag fothering plugs are now shipshape and Bristol Fashion, looking like they belong on the *Titanic's* hull.

In the First Class Smoking Room Lord Peter lingers for a last brandy with the barmen, Parker and Collins.

"Astonishin', me lord. Imagine savin' this big, modern ship with fotherin'. I 'eard about it from the old salts, but never thought I'd see it. I wager it hain't been done in a 'undred years." Collins raises an eyebrow at Lord Peter. "I wonder who thought o' that, now?"

"No idea, Collins, no idea," Lord Peter says. "Now, how about that brandy?"

✝

Pops
James Gallahan

When did I get home from the hospital and who put me in my rocking chair on the front porch? I don't remember leaving the hospital. My daughter, Sarah, is sitting in the chair next to me smiling, but her eyes look red and puffy as she wipes away a tear. She must have driven me home.

"So, did you bring me home, Sarah?" I ask. "I can't remember."

My baby girl stares at the clouds deep in thought. She starts biting her lower lip—something she's always done when she's upset. Sarah's probably worried whether I'll be okay after my heart surgery. I call her my baby girl even though she's thirty-five. She'll always be my baby girl.

"Sarah?"

"I'm sorry, Pops. Um . . . yeah. I brought you home. How're you feeling?"

"Tired, but glad to be out of there. I hate hospitals. The smells. All the sad people. I keep remembering your mom's last days there."

"I wish you didn't have to go through all that, Pops."

"That's life."

I notice that the grass is freshly mowed and there isn't a weed in sight. The American boxwoods are trimmed to perfection. There's even a new birdbath in the front yard. "Didn't take long for the Realtor to put up the 'for sale' sign in the yard."

"That's what you wanted, right?"

"Yeah. Just can't believe I'm selling the place. Your mom and I've lived here thirty-six years. But it doesn't make sense for me to stay here all alone

96

in this big house." I give Sarah a teasing grin. "You're sure you, Tom and the kids don't want to live here with me?"

"Thanks, but no, Pops. We've been over this a bunch of times. We can't drive two hours to work each way. Plus, the kids have their friends at school."

Sarah's right, but that doesn't change how I feel.

"I know," I say in an old creaky voice. "I was hoping you'd take pity on your old man, especially after he suffered a massive heart attack."

"Very funny, Pops."

I tap my chin as if a thought just hit me, and then clap my hands. "How about I stay with you?"

"Pops, we've also been over that one a bunch of times. Our place is too small. We're busting at the seams as it is. The kids would drive you crazy. You know how tired you get after spending an afternoon with all of us."

She's right again. But I don't like it.

"I'm sorry, Pops."

"It's getting cold." I frown. "Let's go inside."

"You're going to love how the Realtor's staged the place."

I walk inside and just stand there looking wide-eyed at what they'd done. *A fresh coat of white paint and new crown molding makes it look like one of those expensive houses in the new section down the road. I can almost see myself in the floors.* I smile at Sarah. "I can't believe it's the same house. It's never looked better."

"Looks good, huh?"

"Sure does. They did a fantastic job. Maybe I won't sell after all. It's too nice to leave now."

"Yeah right, Pops."

We walk into the garage. My favorite place to escape. I scrunch my eyebrows and raise my hands. "What'd you all do with my stuff?"

"Sorry. It's in storage. The Realtor thought the garage would look bigger if we took out the tools."

"Guess so." I shrug my shoulders and look down at the floor.

"What's the matter, Pops?"

"I knew this day would come. Just thought I wouldn't be here to see it. Figured I'd go first. Your mom was always the healthy one. I had the heart problems. But I guess cancer even gets the ones taking care of themselves."

"I'm sorry, Pops."

"How 'bout you fix me some ice cream? Maybe that'll cheer me up. Nothing like a banana split with extra nuts and whipped cream to brighten my day. I'm sure Doc Murphy would have a fit, but he doesn't have to know."

"Sounds perfect."

I sit at the kitchen table squinting my eyes, trying to get things in focus. My ears keep feeling like they're clogged up. Everything's a little bit muffled. Guess those drugs they gave me during surgery are still in my system. I end up not eating the ice cream. "Sorry, I don't feel like eating anything. How about you put it in the freezer?"

"Sure thing, Pops. You've been pretty quiet. You okay?"

"Yeah. I think I'm still a little loopy from the surgery." I force a smile. "I was thinking we could drive up to the mountains and stop by the cemetery to see your mom."

"Oh, I don't know, Pops." Sarah gazes out the kitchen window. "You've been through a lot lately. Don't want you to get upset. How about we go this weekend? It's only a couple of days from now."

I shrug. "You're probably right. But you're staying with me the next few days, right?"

"Absolutely. I won't leave you until you're ready."

"Are Tom and the boys coming over?"

"No. I told them to give us a few days. You know, so we could catch up on things."

"Okay. But I miss those boys. You've done a great job with them. I'm very proud of you."

"Thanks, Pops. That means a lot to me."

I yawn like I haven't slept for a hundred years. "I think I'll go lay down for a little bit."

"Let me know if you need anything."

I end up not sleeping very well. Keep having weird dreams about the hospital and the doctors working on my heart. I'm floating above the operating table watching them perform the surgery. Then I see Sarah, Tom, and the boys sitting in the waiting room. Then I'm back watching the surgery again.

At times I hear my wife, Bridget, speaking softly to me. "Don't worry Seamus, my love. They're good doctors." Then I hear her snicker, "No more cheeseburgers for you."

I wake up and walk into the living room. Sarah's sitting in my usual chair—or what she calls "Pop's chair"—crying. "What's the matter, sweetie?"

"Oh, nothing."

"Come on. You can tell your old man anything."

"I'm just worried about you, Pops."

"I'm fine. My ticker's good as new. I ain't going anywhere soon. You can't get rid of me that easily."

"I just want what's best for you. I know Mom misses you a lot."

"You been having those dreams about your mom?"

"Um . . . yeah."

"I miss her, too. We'll be together again one of these days. But I still have a ton to do. Gotta sell the house. Get settled in my new place at the retirement center. Probably sell the car, unless you want it. Timmy's graduating from high school next June. I can't miss that."

"I'll take care of all that, Pops. You can just let it go."

"Can't have my baby girl doing so much. You got plenty to do without worrying about me. I love you for wanting to take care of me, but I got it." I give her a big smile. "Like they say, I can rest when I'm dead."

99

"Okay. I'm gonna head up and go to sleep. I'm pretty tired."

"Good idea." I walk over and kiss her forehead. "I'm going to go over the estate papers one more time. Want to make sure I didn't miss anything. I promise I won't overdo it."

"Goodnight, Pops. I love you."

"Love you, too."

I stay up another hour going over the documents. I changed my will and power of attorney when Bridget passed, and I want to make sure everything is just right. Don't want Sarah to have to worry about that stuff when I die. I wake up the next morning to the smell of bacon and eggs cooking.

"Smells good. You made my favorite."

"Mine, too. Want a plate?"

"I'll have a little bit. My appetite's not back yet." It takes all my strength just to lift the fork. "Maybe I'll have something to eat later."

Everything still looks fuzzy. Seems to be getting worse since I got back from the hospital. My hearing's getting worse, too. They didn't give me any medicine to take home with me, so I know it's not that. Probably just the effects of the anesthesia.

"Let's go sit on the porch in the backyard," Sarah says. "It's beautiful outside."

"Sure, but not for too long. Sorry, I'm getting tired again."

It's a gorgeous day. I lift my head to soak up the sun and feel the gentle breeze brush across my face. Butterflies land on the buddleias we planted for them. Cardinals perch on the birdfeeder eating sunflowers seeds. I can't remember seeing so many cardinals and butterflies. They're everywhere. I thought a monarch was actually going to land on my shoulder. I look at Sarah wide-eyed. "Did you see that?"

"I know. There seems to be a bunch of butterflies flying around today. I was thinking . . . you mentioned going to the cemetery."

"Yeah. Let's go see your mom. We can go now if you want."

Sarah takes a deep breath and then wipes away a tear. "Let's do it."

It takes us an hour to drive up to the cemetery. Sarah and I sing songs. We play those silly license plate games. She lets me win. Sarah sheds a tear every now and then. Going to see her mom still upsets her. She misses her a lot.

"How about we go in through the hillside entrance, Pops. I think it's a nicer view."

"Yeah. I like that way better. You look upset. I know it's tough on you seeing your mom here. Sure you want to go? I can go by myself."

"No. I hate doing this, but it's for the best."

"What's for the best? Seeing your mom?"

"Um . . . yeah. Sorry, I'm just upset."

"I understand, sweetie. We'll stay for a little bit and then head back home."

We walk hand in hand down the hill toward Bridget's headstone. A few more butterflies flutter around us again. I even see some more cardinals flying toward us.

As we get closer, I see that the ground next to Bridget's grave was recently excavated. There's a headstone there, too.

"Looks like they just buried someone recently, huh?" I look at Sarah and scrunch my brow. "That's strange. I thought your mom and I were the only ones to be buried in this section."

Sarah looks down as she walks. She doesn't say anything.

I try to lighten the mood. "Guess your mom and I are going to have neighbors."

Sarah doesn't say anything, but starts to cry.

"Let's leave. This is upsetting you too much."

"I've got to do this, Pops. Please look at the headstone."

"Okay." I walk around the other side. The tombstone reads "Seamus Timothy O'Reilly." I clench my hands and grit my teeth. "What's going on? Is this someone's idea of a joke?"

Sarah wipes away tears and bites her lower lip. "I'm sorry, Pops. I wanted to break this to you gently, over time. I was trying to do the right thing. I wasn't trying to trick you or lie about what happened. You didn't want to let go yet. You still wanted to take care of everything. I just wanted to ease you into what I knew would be painful for you . . . and for me."

I rub my hands over and over, and shake my head left and right. "Okay, if I'm really dead, then how am I talking to you like normal?"

"You know how I used to tell you, when I was young, that I could talk to spirits?"

"Yeah. We all thought you were just trying to get attention."

"Well, I really can see and talk with people who have and haven't crossed over yet. Mom and I talk all the time. She's right over there by the oak tree. She's waiting for you."

I can't turn around. I won't turn around. "Yeah, right."

"Please, Pops. Look over there."

Slowly, I look toward the tree. Bridget is standing there. I fall to my knees and close my eyes. It feels like minutes before I open them again. She smiles and walks toward me. I can't move. I can't do anything but stare at her.

"Hi, sweetheart," Bridget says. "I've missed you."

I look at Sarah. "Is this real?"

"Yes, Pops. Speak to Mom."

"Hi, honey. I don't understand what's going on. I must be dreaming."

"Sweetheart, I love you so much," Bridget says. "It's time for us to be together again. But that can't happen until you let go of the things that are keeping you here. Sarah will take care of everything. You don't need to worry about it anymore."

"But I'm not dead. The surgery made me better than ever."

"No, darling. The damage to your heart was worse than they thought. The doctors tried to save you, but your heart just gave out."

"But I came home after the surgery. I don't remember how, but Sarah said she brought me home."

Sarah glances at me and then looks down. "Your body was here at the cemetery, but your spirit was at home, Pops. Tom took care of the funeral arrangements. I was at your burial when you were sleeping yesterday. I tried to ease you into coming here."

My eyes dart back and forth between Bridget and Sarah and the grave. "I just need a few more days. Then I'll come back here. I really do miss you, sweetheart, but I can't just up and leave. I've got to sell the house and get everything in order."

"Seamus . . . you know all the butterflies and cardinals you've been seeing?" Bridget asks.

"Yeah, I've never seen so many."

"I was sending them to you as a sign. It's time, Seamus." Bridget points up the hill. "It's time to go toward the light over there."

"I see it. It looks beautiful."

"It is, sweetheart. You'll love it. No more pain. Just peace and joy from now on. Forever. Your mom and dad are in the light, too. They can't wait to see you. Take my hand. I'll go through it with you."

I look at Sarah. Tears fill my eyes. "I can't leave you, Sarah. You're my baby. I'll miss you too much."

Sarah cries, but talks as her chin trembles. "Remember, Pops, I can still talk with you. I've got that gift. We'll never be apart. I think you should go with Mom. It's time."

"You sure?"

"Yes, Pops."

"I'll always love you, baby girl."

"I'll always love you, too, Pops."

I take a deep breath, hold Bridget's hand, and walk toward the light.

✝

Pyramid Scam

Rachel C. Thompson

It was the final gathering.

Long did the elites know that the comet would return and cause greater harm. The Group, as they called themselves, the rulers of the world, didn't tell the populace. Rather, they contrived means to have the people build their refuges as public monuments and works of art. Anything but their true purpose was revealed. How else could one justify such great undertakings? Zebedee thought it was genius to fool the public in this way, and better yet, hiding the Group's true purpose while appearing as heroes of the people was honey on dried fruit. People needed work. The rest of the Group deferred to Zebedee's wisdom.

Each of them had supplied the funds and each family had built a massive shelter, its size proportionate to the family's status. Of course, Zebedee's pyramid was the grandest of all, save the few across the great waters and far south of the ice packs. Only Zeb knew, as the head of astrophysics, that the people across the ocean would not survive. The comet would impact the northern ice sheet.

Zeb and the others stood at their chairs, all plainly dressed in common array. It wasn't safe to go about as wealthy citizens. The people had recently learned of the impact and were roused. The night sky was lit with a new sun and such light opened the rabble's eyes. The jig was up.

"We must now descend into our bunkers; the event is upon us," Zeb pronounced upon sitting.

"But my casing stones have not yet been installed," Trotman said. "I cannot get the workers back, no amount of money will they accept. See how ungainly it looks? They are leaving in masses, traveling to Anatolia."

"Do you not understand?" Zeb was amazed at how shallow they were, petty concerns in the face of disaster. Their gold, their money, their slaves, none of it mattered. "Trot old boy, get into your bunker and have the slaves seal you in before it's too late. As for me, I go this afternoon."

No one had casing stones. They would have to take their chances. And, oh had Zebedee fought for the stones. He had made war on the mason's union to no avail. He was lucky they finished the structure in twenty years. The Free Masons had had their fill a year before impact and the union left for Anatolia before the rest, beginning the trend.

On that last gathering day, the elites ventured underground.

Over the next forty years, Zeb and his kind expanded their network of tunnels and made the best of life below the surface. Only one of their sub-equatorial shelters failed when its nuclear pile exploded for lack of cooling water. The great river had radically shifted its course. That shelter had been far from Zeb's complex and its demise caused him no harm. Although the sky had cleared, and the weather improved year to year, and farming became possible, Zebedee and his kin preferred the safety of their holes as the surface survivors sought revenge. Underground, come what may, the Group would long outlive the memories of this generation. Then, their prodigies would emerge and carry on their reign. Such was the great hope.

৶

Harim was a hero of the people, for it was he who motivated them to depart in time. Before the comet had been close enough to see with the naked eye, he began excavations and others did likewise after his example. Harim had designed the largest of the underground cities where the people took shelter. He had been a young man then. He was old now and no longer hammered and chiseled, setting an example of manual labor as to preserve the laser cutters. He had reserved the cutters for another purpose.

The people had elected him union president, but never again would they trust leaders unquestioned. Everyone had voted. It was then decided that scouts go back and see what they could. The pyramids and much else still stood, the scouts reported, so the effort was made. A force of masons ventured into the ruined world.

Harim eyed Zebedee's monument. Smoke wafted out of his pyramid along with the others. There was no sign of the residents, just smoking vents everywhere in the landscape.

Zackery, the new foremen, asked, "How to pay them what they deserve? This plateau is a honeycomb. We cannot fight them in the tunnels; it would be suicide." He pointed at a laser cutter. "We can't waste equipment."

Harim scratched his beard. "If we use every power pack, we could not cut away enough stone to get them out, true enough. The structures, as I recall, are riddled with hidden chambers. It will take years to find them all and with so many escape tunnels, too. So why bother digging? I say leave them where they are."

Zackery was flummoxed. "How will we take revenge?" The Group had abandoned them to die. The people demanded justice. So many more would have lived if the priest-scientist had given advanced warning. "How, how do we repay them?"

"We fulfill our contract. We are honorable men, are we not? We were paid in advance for the casing stones. So let us encase the pyramids. We thereby remake their sanctuaries into tombs."

"Yes, we have cutters enough," Zackery agreed, "and should we use softer stones, limestone, yes, our power will last the job, and infilling with a sticky lime slurry will plug any gap."

"That is why you were elected foremen. A Free Mason must think logically."

"Do you think they all will perish?" Zackery asked. "They are devious."

"Some may wiggle out like worms on their bellies, yet their power is crushed." Hiram paused and looked up at the great monument he himself worked on so long ago. "We must be forever vigilant, but I trust this ends them for good."

∽

Rachel C. Thompson

Twelve Thousand Years Later

Ned and Mark were arguing as usual at the tourist bar in Cairo, and Ned was getting tired of it. Both Americans were on the German dig team, but Ned was old school and Mark was young with a recent doctorate under his belt. The young man clearly didn't understand the reality of archaeology's situation.

"It doesn't add up," Mark was saying. "Why build a pyramid tomb? Fine, the King's Chamber has a stone box, but how can you say it's a coffin with no supporting evidence? There's nothing on the walls. All the tombs of Egypt we've seen were decorated, had grave goods, texts, but nothing in the King's Chamber, and Queens Chamber, it's not even close."

"Occam's razor," Ned replied.

"Why is it the oldest structures were more sophisticated?" Mark went on, ignoring Ned. "I'm telling you the evidence points to an older, more advanced civilization. What about the precision, the perfectly drilled holes, how'd that happen? The Egyptians didn't even have the wheel. Christ, Ned, why can't you see it?"

Ned took a big pull off his drink and snubbed out his cigarette.

"Look, kid, I've seen all kinds of anomalies in my twenty years of field work. Some stuff's way out there, I'll grant you that. But here's the thing, if you want that research money, the university job, the grants and book deals, you don't put that stuff out there. You don't want to be the next tinfoil hat buffoon, or worse. Look what they did to Lester."

"But what's wrong with the truth?"

"I'll tell you what's true. You play along to get along." Ned put his finger to his head like it was a gun and dropped his thumb like a hammer. "The money men don't want people to know. That's all *you* need to know."

"What are they hiding? Damn it, Ned, why do you always have to talk in riddles?"

A flash memory came to Ned's mind—a thing he would never share with anyone. He'd been about Mark's age and in Nazca when he located a tunnel. It had been a huge discovery since nobody had known there were any tunnels there. It could have made his career. As he stood there at the entrance, a man with a torch approached from the far end. The man was seven-feet-tall with six fingers on each hand and a cone-shaped head that didn't resemble any cradle boarding skull Ned had ever seen. The man's jaws had been massive, but he spoke in a whisper. "If you value your daughter's life, you will leave and never return." With that, the monster had simply turned and walked back down the tunnel—Ned ran like hell and never looked back.

"Come on Ned, what gives?"

Ned signaled for another drink and pushed back his fedora. The man that had been watching him from across the room was still there. The man swiped his nose with his index finger but there was no fly on it. Ned didn't pull his money. Let the kid pay. Education wasn't cheap.

"In this world, there are men in the shadows pulling strings. Call them the deep state if you like, kid, but the fact is, if you cross them . . . Lester is lucky to be alive."

Lester had been on local radio talking about the tunnel system. Next day, he was found in the desert buried up to his neck. He never said who did it.

Ned slid off his bar stool, slugged down his whiskey, pulled his hat down low, and walked toward the door as the man in black moved toward Mark.

"Fine, bury your head in the sand," Mark called after him.

Ned didn't look back. He didn't hold his head high either, but at least it was still attached to his neck.

†

Redemption
Keith Keffer

Hell isn't as hot as you'd expect. I mean it's hot, but that's only because the air conditioner in the office is on the fritz again. It's not even a dry heat. The humidity was so high that I was sweating just sitting down doing nothing.

Well, I suppose it wasn't nothing. I was staring at the black phone in the middle of my desk, waiting for it to ring.

Hell for me was a three-foot by three-foot cubicle with a folding chair and a pink lamented desk. The fuzzy walls were lime green today. Some days they were traffic cone orange or fluorescent blue or some other bright color combination that managed to leave me with a headache until I managed to tune it out.

As soon as the headaches stopped, the color would change until once more it felt like an iron spike was being driven between my eyes. Some days it was like I lived in a kaleidoscope. The colors changed so quickly that I felt like I was going to throw up.

Except I didn't. I would hang there just on the verge of vomiting with that metallic taste in the back of my mouth as my stomach fought to push everything out, while my throat constricted to keep it all where it belongs.

It would all go away once I picked up the phone. It had a ring like a rock being shaken in a tin can, and no matter how many times I heard it, the noise still made me jump. I hated that sound with a passion that I didn't think I could have for an inanimate object.

The damn thing rang as if thinking about it was enough to make it happen, and I jerked back, away from it. For an instant, I thought the chair would tip over backwards and send me sprawling. Instead, it righted itself

109

and slid forward until my stomach hit the desk, placing me only inches from that cursed phone.

Except it wasn't the phone that was cursed. I was, and all I had to do to make things better was to answer that phone and talk to the poor soul on the other end who was desperately seeking help.

Then, I had to make them suffer. It was sort of an exchange service. The more the other person suffered, the less I would. Just picking up the phone would make the headache go away.

"Come on, Bob. Answer the phone." The disembodied voice came from beyond the cubicle wall. It was deep and raspy, and I always pictured it belonging to a big guy in a dirty T-shirt with a cigarette hanging out of the corner of his mouth. Not that I knew what he or any of my other coworkers looked like. I was trapped in my cubicle, and I imagined they were trapped in theirs.

"Answer the phone and we'll get you a new chair." The second voice came from the other side. This one was high pitched and squeaky, like a kid sucking on a helium balloon.

"How about a fan?" asked the raspy voice. "Wouldn't you just love having a cool breeze?"

The phone rang a second time, and the noise hammered at the spike between my eyes. The headaches were always worse when I tried to resist. The chair pushed me even closer to the desk.

"Answer the phone, Bob." The voices repeated that phrase over and over in almost irresistible chant.

Almost irresistible is still resistible. I gritted my teeth and stared at the phone, willing it to stop. In response, it rang a third time. The muscles in my neck and back trembled as I fought the urge to reach out and pick up the phone. I just had to ignore it.

"Bob," said a new voice. This one was soft and gentle. It reminded me of my mom telling me everything would be all right when I fell and skinned my knee. That would be my Boss. He probably had a name, but I didn't know it. To me he was just Boss.

"Answer the phone and your suffering will come to an end. What's happening to you isn't your fault. If that person on the phone hadn't called, you wouldn't be suffering right now. It's their fault. Release your pain and anger on them."

"You did it before," said the helium voice.

"You can do it again," finished the raspy voice.

"Punish them for the pain they caused you." Boss whispered the words, but they were the clearest of them all.

This was Hell. I mean literally Hell or Hades or the Underworld or whatever name you have for the place bad people go to be punished when they die. It wasn't just a crappy job, and I was trapped here.

They were right, all I had to do was answer that phone and make someone else's life miserable for my little slice of existence to get better. The crueler I was the more I would be rewarded. It didn't last though. I had to constantly be cruel and viscous if I wanted my own suffering to stop. It was like being a drug addict who needed a bigger fix each time if he wanted to maintain the same high.

That's the easy path—the one they want me to take, and it's the one that I can't take, not anymore.

There is another path. It's the hard path, and for all I know it's just a myth. Then again, I thought Hell was just a myth until I ended up here. I wasn't a bad man, but I did some bad things. At the time, I didn't think they were bad, just necessary evils. Well, it turns out evil is evil, whether it is necessary or not.

I can't change that. Only a fool or a politician believes you can rewrite your past. What's done is done, and nothing I do now is going to undo my past mistakes. I would be lying to myself to think that I could, and believe me, I lied to myself at first. I wanted to take the easy path. I didn't want to face the truth.

No, I can't erase the things that I've done, but that doesn't mean I have to keep repeating past mistakes. Even in Hell there is the promise of redemption. That's the hard path, and everything about this place is designed to make it even harder.

I'll find a way. I've made mistakes. I need to own them and not punish others for the things that I've done. Today is just one step on that journey, and I have no way of knowing how many more steps it'll take. I just know I can't stop. I must keep moving forward. There is a light at the end of this tunnel, and I will find it.

The phone rang a fourth and final time.

✝

Summer's End
Rory Janis Miller

Genna stood in the tiled hallway outside her mother's room while the hospital staff moved quietly around her as if she were invisible. They were busy going about the jobs that would keep the people inside the other rooms alive, moving in and out of the open doors in an efficient stream. Her mother's door was tightly shut. Genna knocked softly and pushed it open. Once inside, she saw a woman and a man standing by her mother's bed. At the sound of the door opening, the woman looked back over her shoulder.

"It's about time you got here."

"Carly, don't start," said the man. He gave Genna a sympathetic smile and waved her toward them.

Genna dropped her coat and bag onto the recliner in the corner of the room and joined her sister and brother-in-law at the bedside.

"I live in California for crying out loud. I can't be here every day like you can," she said.

"Well, lucky for you that I can, isn't it?"

"Look, I came as fast as I could. I came in on a red eye, got practically no sleep, and had a nightmare drive up here from the Philly airport. To top it all off, after I finally got to the hotel, I had to run out to buy a coat. I forgot how damned cold is still is here in February."

Carly glared at her sister. "You keep saying 'I.' Didn't Mark come with you?"

Genna hesitated before answering. "No."

Carly rolled her eyes. "Oh, don't tell me."

113

"Girls, this isn't the time for your usual crap. Your mother is dying. Have some respect."

The two women stopped arguing and turned their attention to the frail, gray-haired woman propped up in the bed.

"How is she doing now?" asked Genna.

"She's very weak. She's been awake off and on, but she hasn't eaten. She did drink a little, though," answered Carly.

Genna nodded. "I talked to the doctor on my way in. We went over everything. I know it won't be long."

"I'm glad you're on board with the advance directive."

"Of course I am. I know that's what she wants. It's hard enough as it is."

"She's been through so much. Her poor heart just can't take any more."

"I know. We've gotten used to her always rallying and pulling through. But we knew this would happen one day."

"She's comfortable. That's what's important." Carly dabbed her eyes. She leaned in close to her mother and tapped her shoulder gently. "Mom. Look who's here."

Their mother opened her eyes slowly and smiled weakly. "Carly?"

"Yes, it's Carly. But look who else is here." She gestured toward her sister.

"It's Genna, Mom. I'm here now, too, with Carly. We're both here."

"Oh. Together." Her smile grew wider.

"Yes, Ma, we're together. We're both here with you."

"Happy," said their mother as she closed her eyes again.

Carly bent over to kiss her mother on the cheek, then stood up and stretched her back with a heavy sigh. Her husband put his arm around her waist and gave her an affectionate squeeze.

"Now that Genna is here, why don't you take a break?" he said. "We can run home and grab something to eat. Maybe you could lie down for a little while."

"Sounds good," she answered. "I think I do need a break. Will you stay here while we're gone, Genna?"

"Of course. I think Tony's right. You both could use a little time to recharge. I'll let you know if there's any change."

"Okay, thanks. We'll be back in a couple of hours."

"Take your time. I'll be here," Genna assured her. She stood in the doorway and watched as her sister and her husband walked down the hall and got into the elevator.

Genna went back into the room and set her purse on the wide window sill, pushing aside the usual hospital clutter—yesterday's newspaper, a box of tissues, a Styrofoam cup, a TV channel guide. She pulled out an iPod and speaker, pushed a couple of buttons, and placed it on the sill. In a few moments, golden oldies began playing softly, lifting the gloomy atmosphere. Then she went to her mother, kissed her on the forehead, grabbed her coat and purse, and flew out the door.

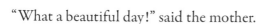

"What a beautiful day!" said the mother.

"What a beautiful day!" echoed back the little girl.

Genna lay in the yellow rope hammock watching the shadows of the maple leaves play across her bare legs as her mother rocked her gently back and forth with one hand. The hammock swung between the only trees in their small sun-drenched back yard, two mature white maples that bathed them in shade. On a low round wicker table under one of the trees a pitcher of lemonade dripped with condensation in the summer heat. Next to the pitcher was a small plate with two freshly baked brownies sitting amongst a scattering of crumbs.

The mother paused her rocking to pour icy lemonade into two aluminum tumblers, one gold and one purple. Genna took the purple tumbler and held it against her cheek, the cold metal tingling her warm skin. Her mother sat down in a wicker chair beside her and resumed rocking the hammock.

"Let's save those last two brownies for your sister. She'll be home from swimming soon."

Late afternoon breezes pushed towering white clouds across the blue sky and set off a concert of wind chimes on the porch. The maple trees and nearby forsythia hedges surrounded them with a cool oasis, while their yard lay in a dreamy stillness that begged for a nap. Sinking down into the tufted chair cushions, the mother closed her eyes and sighed deeply.

"How lovely it is. This is the kind of a day that you'd like to be able to put in a bottle and save forever."

Genna stopped playing with the ice cubes in her lemonade and turned her face toward her mother. She wrinkled her nose and squinted her eyes.

"What kind of a bottle?"

Her mother laughed. "Oh, Genna. You can't really save a day in a bottle. That's why you need to savor days like these. Then someday when you're sad, you can look back on this day and remember how happy you were. You can remember what it felt like and smelled like and tasted like, and feel happy all over again."

"But if you could, what kind of a bottle would you use?"

Genna was not going to let her mother ignore her question. She demanded a practical answer or it would go on forever.

"Let me think. I guess it should be a dark bottle, to protect the sunshine. Big enough to hold an entire day. Something with a tight cap to keep it all in."

Hoping that was enough information to satisfy her daughter, she leaned back and closed her eyes again. No more questions came from the hammock. Good.

Within a few minutes, her mother was fast asleep. Peeking over the edge of the hammock, Genna looked at her mother's peaceful face and giggled. Then she carefully jumped down, stuffed the last two brownies into the pocket of her shorts, and ran into the house.

࿐

Genna slipped quietly back into the dimly lit hospital room. Twilight had fallen and the city lights began to blink on in the distance outside the window. The overhead lights were off, but the one above her mother's bed was on. Next to the bed a nurse was typing notes at her computer station. Genna was pleased to hear the golden oldies floating softly from the window sill. *Good*, she thought, *they left it on.*

Finished with her notes, the nurse turned to look at her. "Oh, you're back so soon."

"Yeah. I just had to run back to the hotel for something. Thanks for leaving the music on."

"No problem. Your mother opened her eyes a little while ago. I think she likes it." She smiled at Genna. "She's such a wonderful person. We really love her."

"I know. And I thank you all for treating her so well. You've been great." A lump was forming in Genna's throat. "Would I be able to have some private time with her now?"

The nurse gave Genna a sympathetic glance. "Of course. I'm done here. I'll make sure no one disturbs you."

"Thanks. I appreciate it."

The click of the door being pulled shut echoed sharply through the stillness. Wiping her eyes, Genna pulled a chair over to her mother's bedside. Behind her the Everly Brothers sang softly, *"Let it be me..."*

"Hi, Mom. I'm back. Sorry, I had to run out for a few minutes."

Her mother lay still, the sheets tucked loosely around her, her hands by her sides. Genna touched her mother's pale white hand gently, then reached into her purse and pulled out a big blue Phillips Milk of Magnesia bottle. Hugging the bottle to her chest she leaned over and whispered, "Mom? I brought you something."

She dragged the chair close to the bed, put the bottle on the tray table, and sat with her elbows on the edge of the bed as she talked softly to her mother.

"Oh, Mom. I just have to let you know that I'm sorry. I'm so sorry that

I've been such a lousy daughter. You were always so good to me and I didn't appreciate it. No matter what you said, I did the opposite. I don't know why. I just did."

She took a deep breath and went on.

"I messed up every single thing I've ever done. I dropped out of college, screwed up two marriages, quit every decent job I ever had. The reason I ran off to California was so you wouldn't have to watch me botch up my life any more. Nothing changed, just better weather."

She touched the blue bottle and ran her finger down its side.

"How I wish I could go back and start all over again and do it right this time. If only we could go back to those happy days we spent together, before you and Dad got divorced, before you had to go to work and leave Carly and me on our own—those wonderful long summer days when everything seemed possible."

Genna sat back in the chair and folded her hands in lap, eyes lowered as if she were praying.

"I was such a spoiled brat. Still am I guess. And I know . . . I know I was always mean to Carly. I blamed her for everything. All because I hated her for being so perfect, so smart and responsible and good."

Sometime during Genna's rambling, her mother had opened her eyes, now shiny with tears.

"Oh, Mom, don't cry, don't cry," said Genna squeezing her mother's hand softly.

She stroked the bottle again. "I wanted you to know that I saved this bottle all these years. By some miracle, I managed not to lose it. I wanted you to know that I saved one of those special summer days, a day with sunshine and lemonade and brownies and love. I saved it right in here. I've looked at this bottle, held it a hundred times, remembering. And it saved me."

Her mother reached out toward the bottle. Genna laid it gently in the crook of her arm.

"Mom, I swear I'm going to change. I want you to know that I'm going to be different, I'm going to be better. I swear it. I promise. I won't let you down. I love you."

She felt hot tears running down her cheeks and wiped them away with the corner of the bedsheet. Her mother smiled at her and tapped the cap of the bottle.

"You want me to open it?"

Her mother nodded. Genna kissed her cheek.

"Okay. Let's open it together."

Genna took her mother's hand in hers and together they carefully twisted the cap.

∽

The room was pitch dark except for the faint glow of the monitors. The sudden glare of bright light as the nurse opened the door to come in startled Genna. In the background Elvis Presley crooned, "*Love me tender . . .*"

"Sorry to bother you, but we've been watching the monitors. Her vital signs are declining quickly now. Your sister called for an update, so she knows. She'll probably be here any minute."

Genna nodded as she smoothed her sleeping mother's hair. "Then I'm going to leave. I've had my time. Now she can have her own time alone with her mother. I'll be in the lounge."

The nurse nodded solemnly.

"My goodness," she said abruptly. "It's hot in here."

She walked over to the wall and checked the room temperature. "Oh my word! The thermostat is set at 70, but it's 85 degrees in here. It shouldn't be this warm."

Shaking her head, she came back over to the bed. She picked up a plate with two brownies on it. "I'll get these out of your way."

"Oh, no," said Genna. "Please leave them."

The nurse gave her a puzzled look as she set the plate back down.

"You can tell my sister they're for her."

Genna got up and turned off the iPod, then went to the door and pulled it open.

"But you can throw that away if you want." She pointed to the large blue bottle on the tray table as she slipped through the door. "I won't need it any more."

✝

A Sunday In April
Rosanne Lamoreaux

I entered room ten and quickly assessed the cardiac monitor hanging over the patient's right shoulder.

"How tall are you?" She asked.

"About five feet nine." I noticed the bridal magazine in her right hand, and how the bright sun glistened off the sizable solitaire diamond on her left ring finger.

"Ugh, I thought so! I can't go by your size for my bridesmaid dresses. You're way taller than any of them, by at least three inches," she said.

I hit the monitor to take her blood pressure, as I verified the solution and checked settings of the IV machine next to her bed. "What are you doing, Caroline?"

Throwing the magazine to the foot of the bed, she tossed back her head, "Ugh, I want to scream! Our wedding is just six months away, and I can't get the girls to agree on a dress. Either they don't like the design, or they hate the color, or it's too matronly, or, it's just a tad too long or an inch too short. For four people I've known forever and thought had similar qualities, their styles are as different as the sun and the moon. I have to find a creative way to get them to mutually decide on one dress. So, as you can imagine, the last thing I need is to be in the hospital for a simple blip on an EKG. This is crazy! There is nothing wrong with me!"

I smiled. "Caroline, don't downplay your reason for being here. Didn't you tell Joe, the ER nurse, that you've been feeling tired lately, and had palpitations before you passed out last night? Don't you remember the cardiologist telling you how you're experiencing atrial fibrillation, and need a thorough cardiac work up? Look up at the monitor—your blood pressure

121

is still low. Even a person as skinny as you are should have a higher reading."

"Pahl-lease, it's just pre-wedding anxiety," she responded.

"It may be. But, isn't it better to spend a little time with us and find the reason behind your symptoms that to have your fiance and parents get all upset when you faint again? You do want to walk down the aisle without a scene, don't you?"

"Okay! I guess you're right." She shrugged her petite shoulders.

"So, let's start over. Okay? My name is Roni and I'll be your nurse for today. I'm sorry that CCU was full but, I think you'll find the SICU nurses give much better care! After all, we are used to people having major surgery, with large incisions and tubes in every orifice, and handling all that fancy equipment that comes with monitoring every organ in the body. We pride ourselves on being the best!"

I extended my hand.

"It is very nice to meet you, Nurse Roni from the surgical intensive care unit." She took my hand and gave me a big smile, "I didn't mean to take my anger out on you! I just hate to be cooped up on such a beautiful Sunday."

"I understand completely. To be honest with you, I'd rather be outside, too, than in here today. Shh. Don't tell anyone I said that, okay? So, is there anything I can do for you?"

"Well you might think this is kind of weird, but could you give me a back rub? This bed is really lumpy and my back is killing me. The doctor, who told me that I can only get out of bed to pee with assistance, had absolutely no idea what it feels like to lie in a hospital bed for hours. Geez, you'd think I was eighty years old, instead of twenty-five! I would really appreciate it."

"Sure, get comfortable, it would be my pleasure. I'll lower your bed. Tell me if you start to have problems breathing, ok?" I said, picking up the bottle of lotion.

We chatted, as I rubbed her back. She was to be married in October to a man she literally bumped into in a café in Manhattan. She giggled as she described the look on his face as her coffee sprayed his expensive suit. And explained her surprise when, instead of becoming angry, he looked down and said, "Well, I'll definitely be a fashion statement in court today!" They had been dating for exactly six months when he invited her for coffee one morning, knelt down, and proposed on the same exact spot where she had spilled coffee on him. He told her coffee may have brought them together, but it was the stains that would always remind him of the day a stunning woman entered his life. And if she answered yes, he was going to be the happiest man alive.

She laughed, "I had no choice but to accept. After all, I did ruin a perfectly new suit!"

I can still visualize her smile and hear the excitement in her voice as she talked about her upcoming wedding. Her personality was outgoing, bubbly, and enchanting, with no hint of fear that all of her dreams would not come true.

I chuckled when she talked of how excited her niece was, when she asked her to be a junior bridesmaid.

"Your impersonation of Anna is priceless. You should take your act on the road! I feel as if she's here in the room with us right now!"

She smirked, "You would think she was asked to participate in the Queen of England's wedding."

As she talked non-stop, I reflected back on the morning report—no family history of heart disease; came to the ER after fainting while at dinner with her parents; low blood pressure, with slight shortness of breath when they laid her flat on the ambulance gurney.

Her mom mentioned how she had been having dizzy spells for the last several months. Her parents attributed it all to stress, and her intense focus on fitting into her size-two wedding dress and her refusal to eat three healthy meals a day. The emergency room EKG revealed occasional atrial fibrillation; justifying the need for overnight observation, with cardiac testing scheduled for Monday morning.

In an attempt to relieve some of Caroline's boredom, I consciously made a mental note to check on her frequently. I walked into her room around nine o'clock with ice water and remarked how the unit census was unusually low. As I rearranged things on her bedside table to accommodate the water pitcher, I said, "You're the lucky duck—you'll be my one and only prized patient for the rest of my shift!"

She smiled, "Well, Nurse Roni, pull up a chair. I can talk forever."

Before I could sit down, the flood gates opened. She sighed as she told me where she went to college, the softness in her voice revealing fond memories. Upon graduation with a degree in English, she felt it was worthwhile to obtain her Masters, which proved to be the right choice. Within a month, she was offered an executive position with a publishing company in New York City. She currently lived in Queens, and was home for the weekend to celebrate her Dad's birthday. Without any hesitation she described her siblings and her only niece, the flowers she had selected for the church, her fiance and his family, and how glad she was that her Mom had advised her to hire a wedding planner. She even mentioned how many children she hoped to have someday; acknowledging how blessed she felt that Jeff's salary would make it possible for her to stay home for a few years with the kids.

The morning passed quickly and without incident. Before we realized it, I heard the lunch trays being passed out, and announced it was time for both of us to eat.

A half hour later, I entered her room, "Hi! Did you miss me?" As I reached for the empty tray, the monitor alarms started to blare, lights flashing like a medieval bellman heralding tragedy. I quickly checked her EKG leads for placement, assuring none had fallen off, but her monitor showed a small blip in the rhythm, and then, a straight line.

In that split second the image of pomp and circumstance, which Caroline and I had discussed earlier, was gone. My own heart beating rapidly, as I pulled the cord announcing the code and started heart compressions. Silently praying for her to respond, I ignored the small voice in my head saying it was going to be an act in futility. Every fiber in me believed that, since my peers were on their way to assist, she would survive; after all, I would trust them with my own life.

Sixty-six minutes later, I heard the dreaded news. "She's gone," Dr. Mark said, with a tone of finality, as he looked up at the clock, ripped off his blue gloves and flung them harshly into the biohazard container in the corner. "Call the code for 1345 and notify the coroner."

My mind swirled with thousands of emotions, as I sank to the floor. "How did this happen? We were just talking and laughing; she had no complaints and appeared to be fine." My face felt like an iron mask of excruciating pain. My speech slow and slightly slurred; my eyes struggling to stay in focus, tears began to escape.

"These things happen," Dr. Mark answered quietly, as he attempted to lessen my pain. "I've seen it before—no specific forewarning. The patient is fine one minute, and not breathing the next. It's part of the job that one never gets used to, especially in those so young and full of life and hope. I'm sorry. We all tried our best."

As I looked around in disbelief, instead of seeing a beautiful woman in her white wedding gown, as she had so vividly described a few hours earlier, all I saw was blood. Bright red blood was spattered everywhere in the room —on the patient, the bed linen, the floor, and even on my own scrubs. In our vain attempt to revive her dying heart, Mark had performed an open heart massage. (A procedure that splits the sternum in half, allowing a surgeon to see the heart, touch it, and manually perform compressions in order to perfuse it.) Within seconds, he acknowledged what everyone in the room expected—she couldn't be saved. His tone was filled with sorrow and regret, reflecting the general feeling of all in the room, as he removed his hand from inside her chest cavity.

"Her heart is like a stone; it's hard and stiff. I'm unable to constrict it. I can't get the blood to flow again. There's nothing more we can do for her."

In that precise moment, as I stared at her lifeless body, one question kept running through my mind—how could such a kind and gentle person have a rock for a heart? It made absolutely no sense.

I heard my co-workers offers of condolence as they left the room, although their words sounded muffled, as if they were talking through thick fog. My body felt paralyzed, unable to respond. Dr. Mark silently approached and extended his hand to assist me in rising from the floor. He must have known that this was not the time to discuss the cause. The opportunity would come later, (after the coroner's diagnosis of amyloidosis was shared with the staff), after I had a chance to grieve. All he could do was hold me, hoping his few words of comfort would start the healing process, and eventually eradicate some of my sorrow.

Caroline had been full of passion from the first moment I met her. As I received her report at seven o'clock that morning, I had no idea I'd be her sole companion in the last few hours of her life. Or, that I'd be teasing her one minute and calling the code the next.

My heart still mourns when I envision her cold, lifeless body; her beautiful eyes no longer twinkling with happiness. Yet what has impressed me the most, what has stayed with me all these many years later, is the serene look on her face. Apparently, she had no pain prior to her last breath, and had not made a sound or shown any indication of what was about to occur.

The torment of seeing her final heartbeat was passed on to me, the caregiver. She had simply fallen asleep.

✝

Teller of Not-So-Tall Tales
Christopher D. Ochs

"**E**nd of the line!" bellowed a gruff voice above the stagecoach's roof.

Cornelius Browning bounded out of the carriage, satchel in hand, landing on the backcountry station platform next to a waiting young man in coach livery. The planks of the platform—more like an unshaded front porch—yielded under his weight with unsettling groans that puffed out small wisps of dry rot. He squinted under the blistering noonday sun, that just ten miles before was obscured by a relentless gully-washer that poured through two counties.

The surly man riding shotgun on the stagecoach clapped off a layer of dust that adhered in clumps like cactus burrs to his still-damp clothes. With a grunt, he heaved Cornelius's small steamer trunk to the ruddy-skinned porter.

Before Cornelius could say his thanks to the stagecoach crew, the man plopped back on the bench next to the driver, released the hand brake thick as a two-by-four, and grabbed his trusty Remington. With a raspy giddyap, the driver snapped his reins. The horses whinnied a duet tinged with an undercurrent of panic, and the carriage sped off.

"Welcome to *Waci-Gahtei*, stranger," the youth said with an easy grin.

"Where?" Stifling a flare of doubt, Cornelius glanced up at the station nameplate. Painted letters with a hint of shiny borders long since flecked away declared "Gate-Watch." He whooshed a sigh, relieved that he hadn't been deposited at the wrong stop.

"*Waci-Gahtei*. Where ya headed?"

"How do you know I'm not staying?"

"Not too many people stay here, mister. Not since the railroad went a hunnert miles north."

Cornelius pursed his lips with annoyance. The rail to Provo was still not complete, and this coach was the only connection he could wrangle in time for his appointment.

His gut twitched again with a troubling realization. He looked after the fading dust trail left by the stage, then rubbernecked the length of the one-horse town. The youth and he were the only souls amid the rows of dilapidated buildings facing each other along the main line.

Cornelius looked askance at the lad. He was smallish, but too sinewy to be younger than a teenager. And there was something about his accent that Cornelius couldn't place—Navajo, or Cheyenne?

"I need to be south of Provo, Utah, the day after tomorrow for a big groundbreaking ceremony." Cornelius reached inside his waistcoat for the passes and departure times. "I need to catch—"

"Don't worry, mister. You didn't miss it. The Provo stage will be here in an hour or so."

Slipping his hand under one of the leather straps, the youth hauled the trunk past the station's front doors propped open by empty barrels with sun-bleached stenciled labels. Cornelius followed, happy for any excuse to be out of the brutal sun.

"You seem awful sure, son."

"*Wesa*—town folk call me Wes," he said with a half smile.

"Browning," Cornelius returned with a brusque nod.

"I learned the timetables. Little else to do here." The young man clapped the bell on the window counter. Shouldering open the door next to it, he dragged Cornelius's trunk into the murky room beyond. After a few seconds of shuffling and grunting, Wes reappeared with a stationmaster's cap turned to one side. He tore a numbered card-stock in half, handing one part to Cornelius.

"Here's your claim check, Mr. Browning. Do you want me to tag your other bag, too? Hey, you ain't one of those carpetbaggers, are ya?"

"Wrong part of the country—and thanks, no," he patted the side of his satchel. "I have some papers here I daren't lose sight of."

"Suit yourself," Wes said with a shrug. Tilting his head down, his chin almost touched the counter, and he looked up at Cornelius with a mischievous grin and guilty eyes. "If you run into him, don't tell Mr. Smithers. He don't like it when I wear his hat."

"And where would he be? Matter of fact, where *is* everybody in this town?" he asked with a nervous chuckle as he filed the card in the pocket with his tickets.

"He eats lunch at Potter's general store across the way. He and others sit around the pickle barrel, listening to Mr. Redner. He tells his tall tales most every day."

"Sounds dandy. I haven't had a nibble since we left Rock Springs." With a smirk, Cornelius added, "Even if I had the foresight to bring food on the stage, the storm that harried us most of the way jarred my bones sore, and would've turned the cabin into a pig trough."

"Storm, mister?" Wes said, squinting out the east window. "'Tain't rained anywhere near here in over a week."

"It ended about ten miles before . . ." Cornelius followed Wes's line of sight, dismissing the clear sky with a non-committal shrug. "Never mind. If I'm not here when the Provo stage arrives, fetch me at Potter's." He tossed Wes a nickel to ensure his memory.

His bulging heavy cloth attaché in hand, Cornelius strolled down the deserted avenue, scanning the building signs crafted in the same faded and flecked motif. In front of what probably served as both church and town hall, he checked his pocket watch against the tower clock and nodded with approval.

Cornelius clomped up the landing of Potter's General, shaking off the accumulation of street dust. Nosing past a door propped open with the ubiquitous faded barrel, Cornelius heard a reedy voice.

"He ignored everyone's advice, even the dire warnings from Pecos Bill . . ."

He pushed open the rickety screen door, and walked into a setting he had seen in many a small town during his business travels.

A burly man in an apron tied over a striped shirt with sleeves rolled up, fussing over shelves laden with a cornucopia of dry foodstuffs and sundries. A farmer draped in baggy coveralls, his clodhoppers caked in dried muck and propped up on a disused potbelly stove. A blacksmith still wrapped in his leather apron, sitting next to an angled door, opened and leading into a dark root cellar. A man with a coach company jacket draped over the back of his chair, washing down hardtack with a bottle of sarsaparilla.

Next to the pickle barrel sat a peculiar man with a handlebar moustache. Wobbling to and fro in a rocking chair, his elbows rested on the wooden armrests with his hands steepled in front of him. Dressed in Sunday-go-to-meeting clothes, he rattled away in a hypnotic singsong voice with his eyes closed.

". . . until that fateful night in Ford's Theater, where President Lincoln met his untimely end, by the hand of John Wilkes Booth, firing the bullet forged from John Henry's steel drill."

"What kinda tall tale is *that*, Redner?" piped up the farmer between the others' hoots. "John Henry, maybe. I might even swallow Paul Bunyan watching the play through the *thee-ay-ter* windows. But assassinatin' Mr. Lincoln?"

"C'mon ya old coot," chimed in Mr. Smithers after he wiped spatters of sarsaparilla off his chin. "Everyone knows he's wrappin' up his third term and stumping for his fourth."

The storekeeper failed to stifle a nervous chuckle.

With a wag of his index finger, the blacksmith added with a smirk, "Don't let them *federales* hear such talk. They show up unexpected-like, and don't cotton to traitorous stuff'n'nonsense like that."

"But, Lincoln *was* killed in Ford's Theater," Cornelius blurted out.

Everyone turned their attention like a pack of startled wolves on the unannounced stranger. Redner's eyelids snapped open. After a moment, a friendly grin erased his slack-jawed expression of bewilderment.

"It's common knowledge that Ulysses S. Grant is president now," Cornelius continued, his certainty dwindling with each word. "Right?" he squeaked, his eyes dancing across the nonplussed faces around the room.

The store erupted with laughter.

"What, 'Ol' Piss-Pantsy Grantsy'?" roared the farmer.

"That old sot? Who dragged out the war to a tie?" The blacksmith doubled over, slapping his knee.

"Tie?" Cornelius mouthed in silence.

Redner wasn't laughing. Instead, he drilled dead-serious eyes at Cornelius, who furrowed his brow, full of disdain at these ignorant yokels.

The steeple clock chimed the hour. The farmer, blacksmith and Smithers got up, tired resignation silencing the last of their guffaws. Smithers donned his railroad jacket while the others moseyed out into the harsh sun. He stopped in front of Cornelius, picking the last of hardtack from between his teeth.

"You must've gotten off that last coach, Mister . . ."

"Browning," he said mechanically, shaking Smithers's hand.

Smithers eyed Cornelius's satchel with a mite of concern. "Didn't Wes take care of your belongings? I swear, if that Injun's slackin' off again, I'm gonna beat the tar outta him. And he better not be wearin' my hat!"

"No, my trunk's at the station. Got the claim check right here," he replied, patting his vest pocket. "Wes promised to collect me when the Provo stage arrives."

Smithers gave Cornelius a curious look that almost became a wince, before shuffling out of the screen door.

"Mr. Potter," said Cornelius, "I'd appreciate a bottle of that sarsaparilla, and something softer than Smithers's hardtack, please? My teeth are still jangling from my coach ride in that wangdoodle of a storm."

"Storm?" came the store owner's disembodied voice, followed by a pop of a bottle top. "'Tain't been a lick of rain since I dunno when. We could sure use it, though. The town well's fixin' to dry up."

"Never mind him," Redner said with a dismissive wave of his hand. "He ain't attuned to such things, though *I* could feel the storm . . . worlds away." A wry grin spread under his waggling moustache. "It told me you were coming."

Potter draped an old newspaper on top of the pickle barrel lid, along with a brown bottle and a slab of meat with crumbling cheese between hunks of sourdough. He asked for two bits, and Cornelius dug a quarter dollar out of his waistcoat.

Facing Redner, Potter clamped his hands on his hips and chided, "Now don't you go fillin' my customer's head with yer nonsense." He scolded Cornelius with an indecisive frown, then disappeared again behind his shelves.

Between munches of dry food and gulps of sweetened root tea, Cornelius shook his head and asked in a hushed tone, "What kind of news do these locals get out here? They still think Lincoln's president."

"Well, he *is*," Redner said with a half-grin as he rocked back and interleaved his fingers. "For them—and anyone else here in Gate-Watch. But you and I, we know different. We know . . . sideways from this place."

"You mean, we know better."

"No, I mean *sideways*." Render stopped rocking. "Real for us, but not for them. Our past is not quite *their* past."

"I'm beginning to think Potter's right. You *are* talking nonsense."

"I'm sorry to tell you these things in such a haste, but time is of the essence." Redner leaned forward, urgency in his eye. "It *is* real here. John Henry's real here. Paul Bunyan's real here. Seen him myself. Not too sure about the blue ox, though . . ."

"But you said it yourself. President Lincoln's dead."

"Yes, I did." Redner craned his neck toward the pickle barrel. "But that's not what the newspaper says."

With a derisive snort, Cornelius yanked the paper, and snapped open the month-old *Rock Springs Miner*. His stomach somersaulted, gurgling aloud, when he read the headline splashed across the full width of his hometown paper:

President Lincoln Visits Rock Springs!

The rattle of wagon wheels and a faint cry of "Provo!" wafted through the screen door.

Redner rose from his rocker, and bowed with a flourish. "Not to worry, Browning, you'll have plenty of time to adjust. Gate-Watch is a weigh-station of sorts for souls such as you and I. Now if you'll excuse me, I think I have *your* stage to catch."

Cornelius threw the paper at Redner and grabbed his satchel. He jumped out of his seat, hoping to leave Redner behind, along with the uneasy dread curling around his heart.

Redner snatched Cornelius's bottle and drained the remnants. "Hope you enjoy your stay here in Gate-Watch."

Cornelius dashed out of the store, cutting a diagonal beeline across the rutted dirt avenue. Hearing the screen door slam a second time behind him, he turned to spy Redner traipsing off the store's porch.

Following in a carefree saunter, Redner pulled his cuffs and straightened his bow-tie, all the while maintaining his pleasant grin.

Cornelius tumbled, tripping over an unexpected pothole in his path. Scrambling erect with a choking cough and shaking off the dust from his suit, he gaped in disbelief as Redner ambled around the stage, waving at the driver who called out, "Provo—leaving in two minutes."

Redner climbed the steps to the station door and handed Wes a claim ticket brown with age, before clambering into the stagecoach. Crossing the threshold, he uttered an "Aha," as though he had just received a pleasant surprise. He reached to close the door, before Cornelius snatched it open again.

"You fetchin' to steal my ride, Redner?"

Wes heaved a small suitcase up to the driver, then waved goodbye to Redner, who replied with a friendly salute. Cornelius plucked out his own

…aim check, shoving it into Wes's hand.

"You wish to go to Provo, too, Mr. Browning?" Redner scooted to one side and patted the unoccupied seat. "You're welcome to try."

Clutching his satchel to his chest, Cornelius bounded up the running board into the coach.

He blinked with wonder as he instead emerged out of Potter's root cellar.

"What in tarnation?" Without thinking, Cornelius sprinted once more across the street, skidding to a stop in front of the depression that tripped him up moments before.

It was in the shape of giant boot print, with a name scratched in the heel with strokes larger than a woodsman's axe—"Bunyan."

The driver cracked his whip, and Redner waved out the window of the coach.

"Apologies, Mr. Browning, but this is *my* ride now. I'm afraid you've been selected as *Waci-Gahtei's* new teller of tall tales—until this place decides when *your* replacement arrives. Good luck!" He continued to grin and wave until the coach disappeared behind the last building.

Cornelius let slip his satchel and stumbled in a daze toward the station, staring at the faded sign above. He fixed Wes with a pleading stare of incomprehension.

"Gate-Watch is what you white folk call this place." Wes nodded at the sign before handing back Cornelius's errant claim check. "It's the closest your words come to our name—'the place of lost people.'"

✝

Way Back When
Robert L. Martin

Mr. Stevens was one of the fortunate ones, an heir to generations of good looks that were handed down to him. Like a rose rises up through the ground and flaunts itself before the sun, the seed of his forefathers blossomed inside himself and molded his physique, as he rose up and flaunted himself before the ladies.

He attended church regularly, where he met and courted beautiful women and charmed them with memorized Bible verses. This impressed the preacher, even though he didn't know what the verses meant. And, because he had such a sharp sense of humor, he was a lot of fun to be with. He knew exactly how to captivate an audience, mostly of the female gender.

Stevens was quite wealthy through his inheritance, so he could wine and dine women without emptying out his bank account. Good fortune came to him, and he made the most of it.

All through his life, he never married, because he had so much fun trading each woman in for an exciting younger model. The genes that were passed down through generations stopped when he refused to pass them on to the next.

Stevens wasn't about to let past generations dictate his lifestyle. His parents kept after him to get married, but he preferred not to. After all, he had to honor the creed of the playboys: "Do *not* get married and *do* enjoy yourself." Life was a playground to him, and he was having a marvelous time living the life. He never made plans for the future, because he had so much fun living for the present

Good fortune followed him through his life—that is, until his mounting years started turning them away. The older ones still hung ound, but they weren't appealing to Stevens. Now, as he approached his eighty-second birthday, all he had were pleasant memories to amuse himself with and help him forget about his loneliness.

At the nursing home, he would fool the nurses, sneak outside on his own, and go on long walks along the perimeter of the grounds at night. In his mind he was still twenty-five years old. Unfortunately, his body didn't agree. His legs were a bit wobbly, but he wouldn't let that bother him. He fought the years away with his vanity.

One night, he walked outside the perimeter and followed a path that led into the dark woods. While walking along the path, he looked up and started yelling and cursing at the sky.

"Why have you let old age weaken my legs? Why did you send the beautiful ladies away from me? Why can't I stay the way I was fifty years or so again? Why do you torture me like that? I'll give anything to be like that again. Can't I go back in time? Can't you hear me up there?

A moment later, a big, eerie red face with no body attached to it, appeared in a burning bush. Stevens got scared and started to move away, but his curiosity told him to turn back to it. In a deep penetrating voice it said, "If you give your soul to me, I can help you return to your youth. All you have to do is swear your allegiance to me. I am on your side. I want you to be young again. I can send you back in time."

"Yes, yes! I'll do anything to go back again," Stevens said. Then he heard a deafening noise, thunder-like.

Stevens blacked out and came to in total darkness. His heart pumped at a furious pace, as he stood up and screamed at nobody but the frigid air that engulfed him. His whole body was shaking. "Is there anybody out there? Is this a dream or a nightmare?" He looked around. "Who turned out the lights? Why can't I see? Did I go blind?" He couldn't even see the outline of the sky. "Am I in a room? I'm so-o-o cold." His feet were getting numb.

He felt young again, but couldn't see his new body. In his frantic state, he shouted at the top of his lungs, "What happened to me? What did I do to deserve this? Will I ever be able to see again, and get warm? Help me

somebody! Please, HELP! Finally there was a fire, so he could
something and warm himself. It was that same burning bush, and that sar.
face of the devil again. He now could see what his hands looked like, his
youthful hands. The face said with that familiar voice, "You wanted to go
back in time, but didn't say how far back. That God of yours that you
pretend to know hasn't created the sun yet. It will come tomorrow. By then
you will be frozen to death."

His fiendish laughter shook the cold desolate earth. The fire went out
and the air got colder, as his egocentric life came to an abrupt and merciful
end.

✝

The Whole Truth
Donna Brennan

I just got off the phone with 911. They wanted me to stay on the line until the police arrive. But my ears are still ringing from the blast and I need to get my story straight before anyone gets here.

So I hung up.

The phone in my hand vibrates. It's 911, calling me back. I place the phone on the nightstand next to the gun—the gun Gordy had bought for protection.

 ⁓

Okay, here's what happened . . .

Gordon was taking meth. At least, I think it was meth. He's never abusive, except when he's jacked up on meth. He was starting to crash down and was craving more drugs. I told him there wasn't any more. I didn't tell him I had flushed his stash down the toilet.

He said if there weren't any more drugs, to give him money so he could buy more. He wanted me to call his dealer, Jeremy. I hate that jerk, and what his poison has done to my Gordy. So I said I didn't have any money.

Gordy didn't believe me. He started pushing me around, hard. I bumped into furniture and fell over a few times—that's why the dining room table is overturned and everything's a mess. I tried to run out the front door, but Gordy grabbed me and dragged me back into the apartment, leaving the front door open. He threw me toward the sofa, but I fell on the coffee table, smashing it into three pieces and breaking my arm. At least I'm pretty sure it's broken.

138

I got up and ran into the bedroom, screaming at him to stop. I lo
the door to keep him out. But when he's high on meth it's like he has su
strength, and he crashed through the door.

He thought I was hiding the money in my bra—seriously, who does
that?—and he started tugging on my shirt, trying to get it off me. But that
was hurting my broken arm, so I pulled away and my shirt ripped. I yelled at
him for that, but he said if I didn't give him the money he'd kill me. He had
a crazy look in his eyes. I thought he was gonna follow through on his
threat.

Gordy kept a gun in the bottom drawer of his night stand—he was
always afraid someone would break in and steal his stash. But now, with my
life in danger, I yanked that drawer open and pulled out the gun. It was
heavy, but I held it with two hands and pointed it at him. I was only trying
to scare him, and my left arm was in so much pain it was hard to hold that
thing. I thought the sight of the weapon would get through to him, that it
would make him stop.

But it just made him angrier. He was like a mad man. He raised his
hands, screamed, and came running at me.

I didn't realize I had pulled the trigger, even as the sound blasted in my
ears and I saw him stop and crumple to the ground. As he lay there, he
twitched once or twice, and then stopped.

That's when I realized what I had done. I called 911. It was self-defense.

The phone is still vibrating; I can barely hear it buzz as it shakes on the
nightstand, dancing closer to the gun. I try to ignore both the phone and
the ringing in my ears as I stare at Gordy's limp body. He didn't mean it. It
was the drugs. He was only like that when he was on meth. And now the
police and the newspapers and everybody are gonna think he was a druggie.

∽

Okay, okay, here's what happened . . .

Gordon wasn't home. He only recently bought the meth, but had never
actually used it. Someone must have found out about it, and thought he

ght still have some in the apartment, Gordy's dealer, Jeremy, must have en the one who told this low life about the meth and then gave him our address.

So this guy busted into the apartment wearing a mask so I couldn't see his face. He demanded I give him the meth. I told him I didn't know where it was, but he didn't believe me. He shoved me around, messing up the place, breaking the furniture and my arm.

In the middle of all this, Gordy walked through the front door, saw what was going on, and rushed to save me. He started fighting with this guy. I was certain this creep would kill us both, so I screamed and ran into the bedroom for the gun. The creep followed me in there. I opened the drawer, grabbed the gun, aimed it at him, and shot.

But he ducked, and I got Gordy instead.

The guy ran out of the apartment and I called 911. It was an accident.

But that doesn't explain why Gordy would have drugs in his system. And can they tell if he's been using for a while?

I don't think the screams in that story line up with what the neighbors might have heard. And I forgot to explain the broken bedroom door.

My left arm is throbbing just above the wrist. I can see a bump under my skin, where one piece of bone is sticking up where it doesn't belong. The phone continues to buzz, so I shove it under a pillow on the bed with my right hand.

I hear the police sirens outside. They will be here any minute. Could I be charged with involuntary manslaughter?

⌇

Okay, okay, okay, here's what happened . . .

Gordon had only used drugs a few times, and tonight was one of those times. He was coming down from his high, and went to the bedroom to sleep it off. Right after Gordon flopped down in bed, this huge guy wearing a ski mask busted through the front door demanding drugs and cash. It

sounded like it might be Jeremy's voice. Jeremy is the guy who supp
Gordy with the drugs.

The giant pushed me around and knocked things over, broke my arm, ripped my shirt, and smashed the coffee table. I ran to the bedroom, yelling Gordy's name. I locked the door but the guy crashed right through it, waking Gordy up. They started fighting and I went for the gun, but the big creep knocked Gordy to the ground and grabbed the gun from me. He whacked me over the head, which caused me to fall down on the bed. I think I might have blacked out for a few seconds. When I opened my eyes, I saw Gordy running at him, screaming.

The guy was sitting right next to me on the bed, and he shot Gordy. I saw Gordy stop midstride and fall to the ground. It was awful. I was scared for my life, so I pretended to still be unconscious. I felt him place the gun in my hand and then heard him run out the door.

When I was sure he was gone, I called 911. It was a homicide, and he tried to frame me.

But that won't explain the gunshot powder on my hands. And how would I know what Jeremy's voice sounds like? And the front door is open, but it's definitely not busted.

I hear someone calling my name from the front door. They claim they're the police. Their voices get louder as they approach the bedroom. I'm sitting on the side of the bed, holding my left arm and rocking back and forth. It's about time they got here.

❧

Okay, okay, okay. OK. Here's what really happened . . .

Gordon used to smoke pot every now and then, but never did anything stronger. Maybe coke once or twice. He told me about this guy in the neighborhood, Jeremy—the one who had supplied Gordy with the pot and the coke—talking up meth. Jeremy said it was only addictive if you used it too often, but not if you just take it a few times. So Gordy decided to give it

-y.

It was only the second time he had ever used it. It made him feel so awful that, when he was starting to crash, he asked me to flush the rest down the toilet before he took anymore. He said it was addictive, and that Jeremy must have known that, and wanted to get him hooked. And then he went into the bedroom to try to sleep it off.

That's when this huge masked guy broke in—well, he didn't break down the door, he knocked, and when I opened the door he pushed me inside and asked where Gordo was. That's what he called him—*Gordo*. I told him Gordy wasn't home, so this bruiser started shoving me around, demanding money and drugs. I ran into the bedroom and locked the door behind me. I shook Gordy, screaming at him to wake up. The thug broke through the door, grabbed my shirt, and yanked me away from Gordy so hard and fast, he tore my blouse.

That's when Gordy woke up and started fighting the creep. The mask came partly off and Gordy called the guy *Jeremy*—he asked him why he was doing this. The guy didn't answer, just took another swing at Gordy. That's when I grabbed the gun from the bottom drawer.

Gordy screamed—I think the creep was hurting him somehow. I took aim—I thought I had a good shot, even with my broken arm—and fired. The guy must have seen me taking aim, and shoved Gordy in front of him.

Then Gordy fell to the ground.

It was awful. I called 911. It was an accident. But the thug who broke in was at fault. The police should look for a big guy named Jeremy.

That's my story, and I'm sticking to it.

☩

Winners Write the Story
Emily Thompson

Noon. A light mist glittered Lexton Avenue, Claxton. The C card tableau sparkled on this chilly day. The trial site of Bic needed no decorations or joy or people. Gloss disguised the mist's intent.

Metal ground against the wet macadam, as a manhole cover slid open. A tall figure leaped up and out. Knees bent, it landed with the grace of a dancer, on black wing-tipped boots. He spun once, surveying the street. Standing six foot, he was stocky. But his bulk came from a gray hoodie under a series of Burberry trench coats; he wore over his uniform. Price tags trailed at cuffs and collar. A pair of orange construction gloves and a straw pork-pie hat completed the outfit. His goggled face hid in a wrap of red and green plaid scarfs, worn in deference to the season.

Bunny.

He was quick to jump. No one could leap like him. When he remembers, he'd tell you his name is Connor Drew. But he likes Bunny. Mo always called him Bunny.

10:15, Sunday, December 25, PB, Post Biopop,

Every Sunday morning, fate denounced Claxton. There was no other way to describe it, when Biopop—a sparkly chemical fog—fell and coated the empty streets.

The big three, Big Agro, Big Oil, and Big Pharma, colluded. Their executive concept—a fix that provided a smooth, cost-effective cure for environmental ills. Not by cleaning things up or preventing future disasters. But by vaccinating everyone against side effects of contamination, hence, Biopop.

Bunny grew up in Claxton, a distressed industrial center. He watched it propelled to international center stage. Gritty and loud, and predisposed to ignorance and violence, it was the perfect choice for the macro-vaccination. Lots of money was dangled in front of residents, and the city netted a healthy tax break.

Ecstatic, willing guinea pigs of Claxton celebrated at the Big Three's expense. A full-blown party—open to all residents—a one-time rave to end all raves. Rich, poor, young and old amassed at an abandoned warehouse; the sponsors offered free music and food, plus a fifty-dollar registration bonus. The lucky revelers gathered, glad for their chance; at money and a clean future.

When the party began, the people deliriously stomped the romp. They ate, drank, and danced like there was no tomorrow. The hour grew late, and still, they danced, but now unwillingly. They couldn't stop. What had started as a free-spirited fête, became a compulsive limb-gyrating *danse macabre.* Ligaments pulsed and tendons seized; bone ripped from bone.

Puddles of meat, unrecognizable as bodies, convulsed along the ground. People pleaded for relief. The experts had no answers.

The Centers for Disease Control locked-down Claxton, March 31, 2020. They encircled the town with a twenty-foot-tall concrete wall containing one gate, so no one escaped. Heading off hysteria, the CDC shut down all communication, as well. Silence reigned. Bunny didn't know if they were alone, or if Biopop now covered the world.

Ironically, Biopop successful in the lab, had no documented side effects. But Biopop was never airborne-tested. To guarantee success that Saturday, Big Pharma had salted the sky. The wind-born Biopop transmuted every living thing it encountered.

It became Man's pinnacle of high achievement; cutaneous toxic—that's how the military talking heads defined the drug-fueled mist.

CDC let sanitation engineers in. It was a boon-time for them.

Unknown, they came from everywhere. Native garbagemen like Con. Drew could only do so much, waltzing double shifts, bagging the dead and dying. Birds dropped from the sky, twisted animals, belly-up fish, the citizens of Claxton, all needed disposal. When the CDC packed up and left, locking the door behind them, the sanitation workers also caved to their fate. They joined the piles of carcasses with no one to collect.

But, one-eyed Conner Drew, genetically gifted, side-stepped fate. The dancing garbageman renamed himself Bunny and always suited up, determined to outlast the final romp.

Bunny hesitated, before squishing forward. He headed for Gyllibump's Taproom, his fave, across from Honest Leo's warehouse, Biopop's ground zero.

The neon flickered, bouncing off the burned, black brick of Honest Leo's. Horrified revelers had torched the warehouse on the night of Biopop. Gyllibump's, sandwiched next door, somehow avoided the blaze. Sooty and unlit, Bunny thought it still looked inviting. Gyllibump's had outlived most bar and grills. Over the years, it had survived raids, looters, inspectors and the fire at Leo's. Guarded by steel doors, booby traps, and agitated drunks, the building easily survived Biopop. After all, everybody needed a drinking place, especially after this. Wild stories circulated that a drink from ground zero would undo whatever ailed you, bringing salvation.

It didn't.

Gyllibump's reinforced steel door with highlights of rust, rasped open as Bunny pulled the handle. The mist rolled in with Bunny. Bunny sniffed. Pickled foodstuff competed with carrion. Bunny was unsure which won out. He slammed the door shut, his eyes adjusting to the grim light. He checked the back wall. Mo wasn't working; too early for lunch. Gray shadows cut through the boarded-up kitchen window where Mo ruled.

RULES: BB (before Biopop) customers retrieved whatever food Moana shoved through the crooked opening. Bunny smiled. Mo was a beautiful cooking disaster. Since BB, walking into Gyllibump's and ordering food, was a test of courage or wisdom. Or love.

Mo hadn't been seen in five years. Not since that night Bunny interfered th a customer who hadn't paid for services rendered. The client's shot ook Bunny's eye and nicked Mo. Blood contagion flashed through everyone's mind.

Min reassured everyone.

Everyone trusted Min, even when Mo became a no-show the following night and the next. "Mo just wanted time off to renew her priorities," Min declared.

Bunny wanted that to be true, not some Min bull. Everybody knew Min adored Mo. They were partners in everything. Min couldn't replace her, so by legacy, whoever worked the kitchen, was Mo; one, two, five or even seven, all Mo's. They too disappeared, like Mo.

Gyllibump's, gritty and dangerous, was one of the safest places in the city to meet. But Bunny had no time to dawdle today. When life wasn't so demanding, he could ponder things, but not today. He had a job. Sweeping hair back from his forehead, he brushed stray thoughts away.

As usual, Min was tending the bar. When Bunny approached, her head jerked toward the end of the bar. "Watch that one," she said. "Don't like his looks." Min's low voice a warning. She pulled a draft and set it before Bunny.

Bunny handed Min his hat, two scarves, and flipped back his hoodie. Slipping his goggles up revealed his surviving eye, the right one, crystalline blue. The eye measured the shapeless mass of cloth at the other end of the bar.

Looks like a sack. Bunny would call it Sack. What other names for a mound of fabric perched on a barstool? "Maybe it wants company." Bunny removed his outer Burberry, shaking it out before handing it over to Min.

Sack, aka Brian Vente, creator of Biopop, remained silent.

"Ugh. Do you mind?" Min croaked tossing Bunny's outer coverings towards a toxic recyclables box.

Still gloved, Bunny grabbed his beer and strode towards Sack. "Sack. Bunny." Minutes passed before Sack reshuffled his wrapped portliness toward Bunny. Swiveling back, "I know who you are."

And the bar returned to silence.

Bunny stared, as Sack's shot of whiskey disappeared into the mas
cloth. Presumably where his mouth laid. Bunny hadn't gotten a good look
him yet. His one eye skewed his depth perception.

Sack, with a sloshy sound, slid off the stool leaving a sticky residue
behind. He slammed down his glass, also dripping in something funky. Sack
flipped a silver coin over his shoulder. The coin bounced and rolled, landing
on edge, on the counter. He shrugged his cloth coverings closed and headed
to the back of Gyllibump's, disappearing without another word.

Bunny wondered about Sack. Hopefully, he wasn't looking for the little
boy's room. The public water and sewage system was the first casualty of
Biopop. No bathrooms or running water anywhere downtown.

"Another?" Min asked, grabbing Bunny's glass and pulling the second
draft.

Bunny shrugged, "Sure." The two remained silent. Min, wiping the bar
and Bunny, staring at Mo's empty slot in the wall. "Quiet today."

"Always quiet."

Bunny looked at the coin again. "Okay if . . ."

"Be my guest."

Bunny picked up the silver coin, turning it over. He held it up to catch
the sputtering fluorescent light, then brought it closer. "You know this looks
real. And old." Min shrugged. "No Min. Real old. Like when we were kids
old." Bunny gauged the weight and flipped the coin over. "Seriously Min.
Look at it. It's a museum piece."

Min took the silver from Bunny. She held it up. Then squinting, bit
down on the coin. Her metallic implants indented the coin. She pulled her
Neo medal from between her breasts and rubbed it against the coin. It
didn't stick. She flipped it up in the air, caught it and slapped it flat to the
bar top. "You may be right, Bun-Bun."

"Hate that name."

Aw, it's sweet," she growled. "And suits ya."

Bunny shifted and checked the light now filtering from the front.
Brighter meant the mist had stopped. Mo would be up soon. He knew he

uld leave. His client, Paulie was a no-show.

The Sack hadn't returned yet, and the hallway to the back was quiet. "Think your patron disappeared?"

"Patron," Min repeated. She cracked her knuckles, smiling. "Patron. Long time since somebody used that word around here." Min smiled at Bunny. "Youse always was a good talker," she snickered.

Bunny grimaced and finished his beer, a trickle puddled at the corner of his mouth. His empty eye socket gaped.

Silence, until they both spoke at once. "He's wanting a clean ending . . ."

"Hope he's not leaving a smear on the toilet . . ."

They stopped talking. Then burst out laughing.

"A smear." Bunny pointed. "A smear? Come on, you're worried about a smear? When's the last time you sanitized the back rooms?"

Min dropped her cloth and pressed her gnarled hands on the bar, leaning forward. "That's not the point." She glared at him until she forced her face to relax.

"Want to check on him? For me." Min ducked her head, not meeting Bunny's eye.

Bunny stood up. "If he's 'gone,'" Min continued, "open the trap door," she flicked a finger, "and nudge him in."

"Gone, like," Bunny hesitated, "dead into the sewer?"

"Yeah. Right into the river. *Sploosh*."

Bunny thought a minute. "Seems fitting." And started for the hallway.

"If he has any more coins, they're mine," Min called.

Bunny paused, then disappeared into the dark.

Silence . . . Until, *Squish. Crash. Ugh. Slam. Bang. Splash.*

Minutes passed before Sack re-entered, alone. He shrugged out of his slimy rags, dropping them to the ground. "Piece of cake Ms. Min. That Bunny has a glass jaw. And hits like a girl." Min growled, and Vente looked up. "No offense." He held up his hands. "I'm trying to righten one thing at a time here."

"You know how many . . ."

"I can't fix the dead or the dying," Vente yelled. "Can't fix none of that. He looked away. "I just fix small problems, like the Garbageman. I can't rewrite the past." He pulled a single coin from his heavy bag and tossed it on the bar. "We're square?"

Min stared at him.

"Square," Vente insisted.

"Square," Bunny answered, he recognized Vente. Bunny grabbed the Biopop Wand that Min handed him. The Biopop Wand was a five-foot, pinch point crowbar, a very effective weapon. Min called it her magic wand. When the infected clustered outside Gyllibump's, seeking salvage, Min used the magic wand to shove them away.

Bunny hated the Biopop Wand. It made Mo sad.

Bunny clocked Vente, who collapsed, moaning.

Min stepped from around the bar. "The Bio Wand." She laughed, pointing. "Got the Biopop creator with the Biopop Wand." She doubled over. "So, so fitting."

After she settled down, Min scrambled, pawing through Vente's pockets.

"Looking for this?" Bunny held up the bag of coins.

"Bun-Bun . . ." Min purred, standing.

"You left me to be hacked and thrown down the trap back there. Me, the Garbageman. Thrown into an unfit sewer." Bunny shook his head and tossed the bag of coins into the air.

"Bun . . ." Min stopped short remembering Bunny hated that nickname. "Bunny. I knew you'd survive." She smiled at him. "You're tough, a survivor."

"Really not the point Min."

Min reached backward, going for her gun. "Nu-ah." Bunny shook the Bio Wand. He tossed the bag of coins up again and stepped back. He smiled at Min. "Want them?" Stepping back again and tossing the bag up, "Want

..m how bad?" He asked shaking the bag.

"Come on Bunny," Min snarled, stepping forward.

"Well, come on, then," Bunny said. "Here they are." He waggled them.

Min stretched her hand out, reaching for him. He gracefully, glided backward using the Bio Wand to break the overhead lights. He dodged around the open trapdoor.

"Bunny . . ." Min whined. "I can save Gyllibump's. Can give Mo a proper end." Min extended her hand, "I can get all of us out of here." She held up a crumbled post-it note. "Vente left passwords. Part of his deal to fix things."

Bunny stared at her. "Part of your deal to fix me. You told him I was the Garbageman." He opened his hand, and the bag dropped toward the open trap.

"No!" Min screeched lunging. She tripped, the Biopop Wand assisting, downward to Claxton's dead river. Bunny closed the hatch. Min's screams echoed, as the moving toxic waters overwhelmed her. Briefly, Bunny wondered if Min could swim.

Bunny re-entered the bar and pulled himself a draft. He removed the actual bag of coins and dropped them on the bar top. He studied his reflection in the cracked mirror, and smiled. Brian Vente groaned, rolled over and sat up. "Did you have to strike me so hard?"

"Got the security key?" Vente handed it over. Bunny tossed him Min's keys. "The place is yours."

Bunny rapped the wall. "I hear you Mo." He rubbed his hand next to the slit. A bony hand slipped through, and they touched. Then Mo growled. Bunny jumped up and back, landing on the bar. Mo poked a fork out howling, searching, but not finding him. Brian paled.

"Don't go no place, Mo. Brian's going fix you."

She groaned, her fork scratching the wall. Bunny walked toward the door. "Remember Brian. Rewrite the story."

But I, I can't . . . the past is . . ."

Bunny waved the Bio Wand at him. "Righten one thing at a time."

"What are you . . ."

"Gonna do what I do best. Collect some refuse." He jumped, clickin. his heels together. "One down today. Lots more to fix." His finger scripted the air, *The Garbageman*.

†

A Woman's Fury
Dawn M. Sooy

I heard the chimes reverberate inside the house. My peripheral vision caught the curtain movement.

"Penny, I know you are in there, so you may as well let me in."

The door opened a crack and then widened as a hand reached out, grabbed my arm, and yanked me through the doorway. Before closing and locking the door, Penny stuck her head through the opening and looked left and right. Slamming the door, she leaned against it, skinny arms spread, palms flat against the wood. A long sigh escaped from her lips.

I watched for a few moments, then remarked, "Isn't it a little dark in here for sunglasses?"

Moving away from the door, she shrugged and gave a smile resembling a grimace, walking toward me as if weights were taped to her ankles. We embraced, her a little taller but so slight of form, I could almost feel bones through her clothes. I hugged her as gently as possible. Even so, her body stiffened, and she gasped, unable to control the grunt of pain that escaped her lips. She started pulling away, and I held her hands to keep her from moving too far away.

"Penny..."

Shaking her head, she pulled her hands from mine and sank stiffly onto the couch. I sat next to her and patiently waited, knowing her damaged soul held events of a past littered with unspeakable horror.

Sighing heavily, she faced me and removed the sunglasses, and I saw the remains of a black eye. The once sparkling blue eyes, with promises of the fun yet to come, were now vacant and lifeless. The despairing chill that they conveyed made me feel heartbroken for my friend. Her once-lustrous copper-colored hair hung in dull, stringy strands.

A tear slid down her cheek. I ached to reach out and tell her it wasn't hopeless, but I knew she wouldn't believe me. This had to come from her. She had to take the initiative.

Unable to endure the silence, I asked, "How long has he been abusing you?"

She lifted her shirt. Her skinny torso was marred by the welts from the lash of a belt. Some fresh, others older, as the purple and blue, were fading into oblivion. But they would never fade away entirely, as each mark would always be a reminder. Memories sometimes are more frightful than the vile actions.

As the shirt dropped back into place, she said, "About a month after the wedding. He came home from work before I came home from the grocery store. When I came into the house, he screamed at me, 'Where is my dinner? I knew you would slip up and am surprised you lasted a month, you stupid . . .' He grabbed the groceries and flung them across the floor, and I backed away in terror. He slipped his belt out of the pant loops and . . ."

She was unable to continue as sobs filled her mouth. I slid closer to her and put my arms around her shoulders. I could feel the pain inside let loose with every tear shed, and I tried to wish it away. She cried into my chest until no more water remained behind her lids. After a few sniffles, she pulled away and plucked a tissue from its box and wiped her face.

Silence hung in the air thick and heavy, like a blanket. Penny stood and walked to the bar. Pouring a brandy, she said, "Would you like some?"

"Make it a double."

She poured another and handed me my drink. Sitting back on the couch, she downed hers in one gulp. Then returned for a second round.

"Still at the FBI?"

"Yes, but I'm part of the BAU, Behavioral Analysis Unit. I like it much better than undercover work. We just came back from LA. I had some time off coming to me so, since you've been avoiding my phone calls, I stopped by to find out why. And now I see. I can help you if you let me.

"As I sipped my drink, a tense silence filled the room. It stretched thinner and thinner, and I waited for the rubber band to snap when Penny said, "Less than two months after that first beating, I filed a restraint order with the police, and he punched in the glass on our front door while I was locked inside. They took him to jail that night. The next day he stood at the door with flowers, and he cried while telling me, 'Penny, I love you so much. I can't live without you. Honey, please, I'll do better and go to counseling.'

"I convinced myself Joe's not too bad. When he gets mad, it's always my fault. Everyone loves him, and they tell me all the time how lucky I am. But then just after our one-year anniversary, he pulled me, naked and dripping, from the shower to yell at me because his breakfast was cold. I ended up the floor shivering, unable to move from the beating."

Finishing the remaining amber liquid in my glass, I remarked, "Whatever happened to the spunky girl I called Copperhead?"

As soon as I said those words, I wanted to pull them back the same as a fisherman would with a bad cast. She swallowed her drink, but not before I'd seen the shadowed veil on her face.

When we were in eighth grade, I was overweight and wore the most awful clothes. Not a day went by when a particular bully wouldn't target me on the school bus. Just when I thought I could no longer endure his barbed words and the snickering of his friends, he opened his mouth and sneered the last taunt. Penny stood up and punched him in his mouth, splitting his lip and sending him flat on his butt. I didn't know she could move so fast, much less deliver a punch like that. She was almost thrown off the bus, but when word of the bullying landed on the school's ears, the bully no longer rode the bus. Penny just got detention.

As she placed the glass on the bar, I persisted. "There are ways and people who can take care of problems such as him. I can get you connected."

I knew my words fell on deaf ears.

Before she could utter another word, a key unlocked the door and moments later a man wearing dark blue pants with a matching shirt that bore the name JOE entered. Penny stood motionless and reminded me of a puppy that's been beaten time and again. I swore she seemed to shrink where she stood.

Joe looked at us, narrowed his eyes, and then a grin spread his lips.

"Hi, honey. Who's your friend?"

Penny walked tentatively toward her husband and greeted him with a kiss on the cheek.

"This is Cici Morgan. She is a childhood friend. Her job brought her to the neighborhood, and she stopped in to say hello."

I guess he was too drunk to remember I was Maid of Honor at his wedding.

Years of working as an agent allowed me to perfect a flawless facial expression and body language for any situation. But this time it took every ounce I possessed not to let the rage run rampant as I stood.

"Hello, Mr. Felestnick. It's good to meet you," and my mastery of a fake smile along with the crinkles on the corners of my eyes was impressive if I do say so myself.

"Is dinner going to be late *again?* I don't smell any food."

I saw the grip on Penny's arm and her slight wince.

"Oh, that's my fault," I said. "Penny told me how much you like 'Steak and Ale,' so I've offered to take you both to dinner. My treat. She knew you would be home any moment and I didn't give her enough time to call you at work."

Joe's eyes fixed on my face, and I thought it would crack holding the smile in place. Relief flooded when he grinned, turned to Penny and said, "Looks like we gotta get ready to go eat out."

Dinner was a drawn-out affair. Joe certainly loved to voice his opinion. If I had worn my gun, I would have shot him for calling our waitress "girlie." We ordered a pitcher of beer, and we may as well have placed a straw into it and passed it to Joe. When it was empty, he waved his hand in the air and then snapped his fingers, "Girlie. We need a refill."

Penny's eyes had long since glazed over, and I desperately wanted to stuff my napkin in his mouth. As long as I pretended interest and uttered uh-huh" here and there, he kept talking, so sure he was of himself. After a while, I started fantasizing about the different ways I could maim him, or perhaps make him disappear.

"You're paying that lazy waitress too much of a tip. She's not worth a nickel," Joe slurred and proceeded to take off half my tip and place it in his pocket.

Knowing not to contradict him, I held my tongue. Minutes later we were standing on the sidewalk, and I hailed a cab for Joe and Penny. When they were hustled inside, I paid the driver in advance to take them home.

Please, God, let them go home and have him fall asleep quickly so Penny can have a least a small amount of peace.

I turned and walked back into the restaurant looking for the waitress. She well deserved a much better tip than the money on the table.

Weeks went by, and I tried contacting Penny, but never spoke to her. I thought about dropping by her house but feared my appearance would only ignite Joe's penchant for fists or belts. One night I went home to find a message on my machine.

"Expresso's on Merchant, 9 a.m. tomorrow."

I half expected the tape to end with, "This message will self-destruct in 30 seconds."

I arrived a half-hour early, located a table in the farthest corner from the door, and ordered. I had trouble sleeping the night before, wondering what the meeting would bring.

Precisely at 9 a.m., Penny walked through the door, wearing sunglasses, a large hat, and a cape. She spotted me and slid into the chair in the corner.

Without a word, her cloak slipped onto the chair. Penny's arm was encased in a cast. The hat and sunglasses stayed in place, and I had no doubt what I would find underneath. After the waitress took her order and brought it back, Penny spoke.

"Cici, you had mentioned there were ways to take care of problems like Joe."

I nodded knowing exactly what she meant.

"I'll make the arrangements. You go home and forget today. This way, when the police come, you know nothing. It may take a few weeks, which will be good. You need to keep yourself under control until it happens. You can do it. Freedom always comes at a price."

I purchased a disposable phone and placed an ad on a specific website that said, "The left hand is the past, the right hand is the future." Now I just needed to wait for a reply.

A day later an answer to my ad appeared. "Cthulhu's 10,000 tentacles are far-reaching. The OlD OnE has GReat Power."

I used the burner phone to upload a photo of Joe to the indicated encrypted dark website, ODOE.GRP. In response, I keyed in, "Great Power Grows Stronger After Two Sunrises."

I opened a Bitcoin account with the phone and had two days to load in $10,000. I took the money from my safe deposit box and went to a few different terminals used for such transactions. Each cashier wore sunglass, same as me—the only difference, I wore a wig. A fake camera at each "ATM" took no one's picture. Within two sunrises, the entire amount resided in the Bitcoin account.

The burner phone outlived its usefulness, and I tossed it into a dumpster.

෴

The sniper knelt on the roof of the nearby building and watched as Joe stood outside, drinking coffee. She had trailed her target for a few days before, making sure of the routine. Every single movement burned into her memory. There could be no mistakes. Too much at stake to miss.

This woman's eyes were cold, framed in the passionless face of an executioner knowing this "good old boy" had only moments remaining in his wife-beating life.

Enjoy that last sip of coffee, you worthless piece of human caca.

The crosshairs of the scope divided the face into quarters. No wind blew today. An easy shoot. A moment to savor before the pull of the trigger. Seconds later the head splattered just the same as any pumpkin would. The man next to him wiped remnants from his eyes and started screaming. On the rooftop, the sniper expertly erased all evidence and left the building as a crowd encircled the body.

৽

The evening news of the shooting made the number one spot on all news stations. Penny's family gathered at her house for support. The police questioned her, but could never tie her to the death of her husband. Of course, I stood by her. It also helped that I knew the people from the precinct, as the BAU worked with them on many cases. Later evidence surfaced that tied Joe into a gambling debt with some of the less savory characters of the city.

Days later, I collected the money from the bitcoin account and placed it in one of the many safety deposit boxes I owned. Staring at the heaps of green paper, I wondered how long it would take the FBI to figure out I was the elusive contract killer on their top ten list. Perhaps it's time to transfer the money to an untraceable account and quietly disappear.

৽

To Penny, my dearest childhood friend. As children, we lay beneath the apple tree eating our spoils and speaking of visions our futures. As Maid of Honor, I danced at your wedding and I thought you were on your way to your dream, but instead it turned into a nightmare. I miss you. RIP, Copperhead.

✝

Authors

Rewriting the Past

Sandra Almonte

Sandra is a certified fitness trainer, group fitness instructor, and health and wellness coach. Passionate about the wellness and fitness fields, she decided to try freelance copywriting in 2009. Since then she has helped companies write compelling copy for their products and services both in print and online while still training and coaching clients who are looking for healthier lifestyles.

When she's not immersed in a good writing course or reading a book; she's hiking or on a long walk with her dog. Sandra also enjoys spending time with her other pets (cat and bunny), bike riding, and volunteering for good causes.

You can visit her website at TheWellnessCopywriter.com.

Beatriz Eugenia Arias

Beatriz is a longtime writer, supporter and volunteer in many areas. After writing poems in her early years, she then wrote articles for a college paper, and comments and blogging for human rights issues. Throughout the years she has enjoyed traveling and taking classes. After researching, reading, and writing at home for years, while helping family, she had her first articles published for examiner.com as Allentown volunteer examiner. She then returned to school to refresh her education and shortly after, had her first poem published. She enjoys music, food tasting, walking and photography. Her second poem is on the way, and then who knows, come what may.

Thornton W. Blease

Thornton, a graduate of Sarah Lawrence College's writing concentration and The New School in Manhattan with an MFA in Writing for Children, wants to live in a world where horses and dragons roam free and everyone lives their lives to the fullest. As a freelance writer, editor and associate literary agent he is an active member of SCBWI and travels the country. He as won 26 gold keys and three national titles from Scholastic's Teen Art and Writing Awards and has been published in Scholastic's *Teens' Best Writing, The Underground, River of Words*, and *Common Sense for Animals* journals. Back home in Stewartsville, NJ he visits schools with his dog Ocie to promote literacy through animals. When he's not reading, writing or editing you can find him with his two dogs, five cats, three donkeys, or riding his awe-inspiring horse, Marcus.

Donna DeLoretto Brennan

Donna was a technical writer for over ten years before becoming a computer programmer. Since leaving the corporate world after her twins were born, she's had numerous short stories, interviews, and nonfiction articles published online and in print magazines including *Thriving Family, Encounter, Splickety,* and *Christian Fiction Online Magazine*. Her collection of short stories is due out in March, 2018.

She's a member of American Christian Fiction Writers and GLVWG. She's served in various capacities on the GLVWG board, including several terms as Conference Chair. She's always looking for opportunities to encourage others and to share what she's learned.

Donna's website is www.DegunkingLife.com.

Gail Brittenburg

Gail is an aspiring—expiring writer. She began journalling in her early twenties. Through writing her memoirs she revisited her past and discovered her writing was a form of healing.

Now, at her expiring age, she found her perspectives shifted. Her early journals were written for her daughters to share the adversities of life. Today she shares her stories to let you know you are not alone. You can also overcome life's difficulties.

She was born in a mess and views all of her experiences in life as a gift—story. "Life is one big story . . . good or bad. We learn from every situation."

Gail's memoir collection of lifetime events are written in story format, altered with a twist-or-fate and humor—or Holy Crap moment—if possible. Those who know Gail, know that she will give an honest opinion if asked about decorating, editing, or a life situation such as "Do these pants make me look fat?" If you are fearful of the truth, don't ask. Gail's hobbies are walking, baking, movies, shopping, writing—all fun things in life. She is dipping her toes into the publishing world with her first anthology.

Ms. Brittenburg proclaims, "I was born in Bethlehem, raised in Bethlehem, and because my friends and family are here, I will probably remain in Bethlehem."

Laurel Bruce

This is Laurel's second story published in a GLVWG anthology. She wrote a ghost story for the 2016 GLVWG anthology, *Write Here, Write Now*. Laurel writes children's stories. She also writes fan-fiction based on *The Partridge Family*, *Leave it to Beaver* and *Bonanza*.

Kelly Craig Decker

Kelly has a Master of Science in Psychology. She is a writer/poet/artist who grew up in Bethlehem. She spent much of the last 20 years in the Hampton Roads, VA area where she encountered a number of writers groups. These groups exposed her to a wonderful assortment of people with diverse writing styles and visions of the world. Finding her voice through the support and encouragement of the people in these groups, Kelly had her first poem published in *The Poet's Domain* Volume 31. She recently returned to Bethlehem to continue her journey.

Rewriting the Past

Judy DeCarlo

In nearly six decades of living, Judy has generally played by the rules and has, so far, never been labeled incorrigible. Unlike the boys sent to Glen Mills Reformatory, Judy was born to parents with the means and will to raise her. For this, she is grateful.

Judy has been fascinated by American history and the romance of railroad travel nearly all her life. She's never aspired to jump out of a train, though.

She admits it was a challenge to imagine being Andrew and having the courage to do so. Judy guesses it was a courage born of desperation which made weaving this tale even more compelling.

Judy has had short stories published by *Chicken Soup for the Soul* and the *Misericordia University Literary Journal*.

Judy England-McCarthy

Judy is a member of several storytelling guilds and a member of GLVWG. She loves making up a lot of her own stories and has self-published one of them called *The Adventures of Petunia*, which will be made into an animation sometime in 2019. As a storyteller, poet and author she has shared her talents at numerous events and festivals in both NJ and PA, including the pre-show opener at the Zoellner Arts Center for John Lithgow. One of her original tales was selected to be told at the National Storytelling Conference in 2013, and a video representation of her poetry was shown at The Just Listening Event by the Missouri Arts Council in 2016.

John Evans

John is a long time member of GLVWG, and has served on its board in many capacities including president, vice president, and author advocate. He is also the administrator of the Pennsylvania Authors Network. His first book, *A Tom Sawyer Companion* compares Tom Sawyer's adventures with those found in Twain's boyhood. A short story, *Getting the Bugs out of To Sawyer*, was included in Glencoe McGraw Hill's 2000 Literary Library edition of *Tom Sawyer*. He has also reviewed books for the Mark Twain Forum and has written articles and personal essays. In 2003, his first novel *The Cut* was published by Beachhouse Books. His first mystery, *A Dead Issue*, was released by Sunbury Press in 2013. John lives in Bangor, Pennsylvania with his wife, daughter, and is currently writing a YA novel called *Spooks*.

Bob Frey

Robert is a 77 year old who was conceived, born, raised, lived, and worked on the family farm. After attending the one room Carpentersville school (no running water) he graduated second in his class from Phillipsburg, NJ High School in 1949.

He milked registered Holsteins for fifty years and continued farming until his two sons made him retire three years ago.

His days were spent working on the farm and most of his evenings he was involved with various community activities such as School Board, Planning Board, Warren County AG Development Board, local Grange in Stewartsville, and as a director of the New Jersey Farm Bureau. He has received National and County soil conservation awards and was active in the Antique Automobile Club of America for 58 years. He wrote a column for forty years for the local Old Car Group from which his two-and-a-half books are mostly derived.

Trudy, his bride of 57 years, is a retired home economist, dietician, and quilting expert. His sons live on both sides of their parents and their two grandsons are attending Rutgers and University of Pennsylvania. It is hoped that they amount to more than their grandfather.

James Gallahan

James has a short story that will be appearing in Cat & Mouse Press's 2019 anthology, *Beach Pulp*. He was a finalist in *Writer's Digest* May 2018 Your Story Contest, and won the Grey Wolfe Publishing's June 2018 Monthly Writing Contest. James is currently working on a historical fiction/adventure novel based on the infamous King of Pirates, Henry Avery. He lives in Virginia.

Phil Giunta

Phil's novels include the paranormal mysteries *Testing the Prisoner, By Your Side,* and *Like Mother, Like Daughters* published by Firebringer Press.

Phil's short stories appear in such anthologies as *A Plague of Shadows* from Smart Rhino Publications, *Beach Nights* from Cat & Mouse Press, the *ReDeus* mythology series from Crazy 8 Press, and the *Middle of Eternity* speculative fiction series, which he created and edited for Firebringer Press.

As a member of GLVWG, Phil also penned stories and essays for *Write Here, Write Now* and *The Write Connections,* two of the group's previous anthologies.

Visit Phil's website: http://www.philgiunta.com

Find him on Facebook: @writerphilgiunta and Twitter: @philgiunta71

Keith Keffer

Keith is an author, martial artist, software developer and an avid gamer. His earliest writing revolved around writing adventure games, and three decades later that effort led to the completion of his first novel.

Keith loves books, lots of books in lots of different genres. He tends to be an action/adventure type junkie. If it has monsters, swords, magic, explosions, spaceships, ghosts or cowboys he is probably going to enjoy it. He is also a sucker for crude, twisted humor. Keith claims that it's not his fault. His dad

led him to the dark side many years ago. He tries to keep it reigned in, b~~e~~
it's like the Hulk. Once it is out, it is hard to get it back under control. You
can find out more about Keith by visiting his website at keithkeffer.com or
by emailing him at keith@keithkeffer.com.

Idelle Kursman

Idelle lives with her family in Morris County, New Jersey. She has written
articles for various publications and was a correspondent for a local
newspaper for four years. Her debut novel *True Mercy* came out in
December 2016 and she is now working on her second novel. Idelle loves
attending The Write Stuff conferences and is looking forward to going to
her fifth conference this year.

Rosanne Lamoreaux

Rosanne is a mom to two sons and a daughter, a nurse for over thirty-six
years, a wife of thirty-four years, and a writer and avid reader her entire life.
She lives in Hershey, PA, and has been a member of the GLVWG for several
years. Even though she currently does hemophilia research, you would
quickly discover she loves to tell stories! She'd beguile you with details of
her day, her latest writing project, a curbside anatomy lesson to explain a
diagnosis, or the doing of her kids. For years she stockpiled essays, poems,
fiction and non-fiction pieces, and numerous storylines waiting to be told.
She often wakes up at night, takes a pen in hand, and jots down a line she
heard in her dreams. She likes to include her family in her pieces; they're a
big inspiration to her. She plans to continue writing as long as possible, and
someday to publish her works. For Rosanne, the next storyline is just a
conversation, an unexpected bump in the crowd, or a witnessed scene away.

Rewriting the Past

Robert L. Martin

Robert's writings have appeared in *Mature Years, Alive Now, Wilderness House Literary Review, Poets' Espresso,* among others. He won two Faith and Hope awards for poetry, published two chapbooks, has been accepted for publication in *Pennsylvania Literary Journal,* and appeared in six anthology books. He is also a pianist and the organist at First UMC of Wind Gap, PA for the past 25 years. His main writing influences are Kahlil Gibran and Pablo Neruda. His main hobby is watching the movies.

Rory Janis Miller

Rory grew up in and around Reading, PA. When she was in the fourth grade, her teacher discussed the meaning of the phrase "late bloomer." She decided that she would like to be one and she has done just that. After a lifetime of writing everything from children's books and plays to poetry, short stories, magazine articles, book reviews, newsletters, and romance novels, she finally published her first book, not long after her retirement from her career as a librarian. She started with a short family memoir based on her mother-in-law and a group of extraordinary friends called *Les Amis.* After that she explored her own family life in a heartfelt memoir entitled *BEV:The Invisible Sister,* which centers around her intellectually disabled sister. Since the publication of *BEV* she has focused her writing primarily on short stories and poetry. She is also working on the release of three romance novels written with her best friend Charlotte under the pseudonym of Aurora St. Charles. She now lives in Bethlehem, PA where she writes, teaches Tai Chi, trains dogs, and makes life interesting for her husband.

Darlene McGarrity

Darlene is a Philly girl who dropped out of high school and never thought she'd amount to anything. In 2006, she moved up to Bucks County, PA, got sober, and finished getting her Associate's Degree. Nature is her church, coffee is her elixir, and gratitude is what makes her world a better plac Darlene has three books of poetry published and will publish her first full-length novel in 2019. Despite being a full-grown adult, she still watches Bugs Bunny cartoons, sings out of key to her favorite songs (she sounds so bad . . . someone make her stop), and loves two-lane road trips with her husband and a bag full of unhealthy snacks.

Susan Kling Monroe

Susan is a children's librarian, teacher, wife, mom, and storyteller. She has been writing since she was a teen, and made up stories for as long as she can remember. She is pleased to have this second story accepted for a GLVWG anthology!

Christopher D. Ochs

Chris's foray into writing began in 2014 with his epic fantasy, *Pindlebryth of Lenland*, recommended by US Review of Books. Several of his short stories have been published in GLVWG and Bethlehem Writers Group anthologies and websites. His latest work is a collection of mirthful macabre short stories, *If I Can't Sleep, You Can't Sleep*. His current literary projects include: *My Friend Jackson*, a gritty YA urban speculative fiction; more short tales of the weird; a backstory novella e-book and the second novel in the *Pindlebryth* saga.

If all that weren't enough to keep him busy, Chris designs book covers, was hornswoggled into serving as GLVWG Vice President, and is active in several groups spanning writing, storytelling and anime fandom ("Voice of OTAKON"). It's a wonder he can remember to pay the dog and feed his bills. Wait, what?

Visit him at www.christopherdochs.com, and @Christopher.D.Ochs on facebook.

Bart Palamaro

Bart is the author of one published novel, *The Other Side of Time*, and several published short stories, all pretty much in the SF genre. Almost everything Bart read growing up was SF or fantasy. Even C. S. Forester is a form of SF from a 20thC kid's POV. So that's the only thing he really wants to write. But it has to have a romance of some kind, even if he didn't plan it to. He can't resist that HEA.

Recently he has taken a side trip into Fantasy with the Wentworth series, set in a parallel and congruent Earth where magic works and the occasional crossover occurs. *The Sacrifice, Sorceress Hunt* and *Lord Randolph and the Witch*, are awaiting final editing and publication. His latest push is into the paranormal, with a shapeshifter subculture living and prospering while indistinguishable from anyone else our own world. *In the Teeth of the Problem* and *In the Eye of the Beholder* are works in progress.

Bart is also the TechGuru for GLVWG, riding herd on the web site and various other techie stuff we have to do. For fun and profit he edits and formats books for self-publication, both print and ebook. He also does book covers.

Phyllis Palamaro

Phyllis has been an elementary school teacher most of her working life. She started in NYC, has taught in California and here in the Lehigh Valley. She has been a volunteer chaplain at Phoebe Home, Allentown for the past nine years. The thread that winds through both of these activities is storytelling. She loves to read and act out stories for children of all ages. Phyllis is the author of the Farmer Bonnie series of illustrated children's books, *Farmer Bonnie and Sally the Sad Sow*, and *Farmer Bonnie and Molly the Missing Mule*, and *Farmer Bonnie and Harry the Unhappy Horse*. Phyllis has contributed to the GLVWG anthology in the past. Phyllis is also Program Chair of GLVWG. Its members encouraged her to write for *Lilies of the Valley*, the newsletter of the Parish Nurse Coalition of the Greater Lehigh

Valley, where she is a contributing editor. Her passion is writing inspirational articles about God's hand in the different areas of her life. She still works as a substitute teacher in her local district.

Richard Rosinski

Richard is a successful, published author in many technical areas including developmental psychology, signal processing, speech recognition, and computer operating systems. Now he's switched his focus to fiction examining the different persons that are inside each of us determining who we want to be and what we become. The included short story *Karma Recovery* suggests it's not a simple matter.

Dawn M. Sooy

Dawn grew up in Eastern Pennsylvania and has experienced the four seasons this state has to offer. She received a degree in Computer Science and worked in that field until 2012. Her interests are writing, reading, and fishing.

She is married to her husband, Bob and between them, have four children, two grandchildren, and one great-grandchild. Their youngest son and daughter-in-law are expecting, and the new addition to the Sooy family is due in April 2019.

As a lover of animals, she adopted a Chihuahua named Eddie, a snow leopard, a horse, and a pig. (Only Eddie lives with her, the others are sponsored from afar.)

Dawn has published six short stories: the most recent, *Love Knows No Boundaries* in GLVWG's anthology *The Write Connections*, available through Amazon. Her first novel *From the Darkness*, was published in April 2018 and plans to publish a romance novel in 2019 entitled *Romance Times Two*.

Dawn is currently the 2019 Conference Chair for the Write Stuff Writer's Conference and is Secretary for GLVWG.

You can find Dawn on: www.facebook.com/DawnMScoyAuthor

Bernadette Sukley

Bernadette has been in publishing for over 30 years. She's written and published fiction and nonfiction books, short stories and articles. Her work has appeared in international magazines, including Sports Illustrated for Women, Women's Health and Men's Health. She is a member of GLVWG and served a year as the co-chair for its annual conference, The Write Stuff. She also served a year as GLVWG's anthology editor. She has worked as a wedding venue server, a trauma unit nurse's aide, a local reporter and a substitute teacher at an intermediate unit for autistic children. www.bernadettewsukley.com

Paul Teese

Paul was born and raised on Long Island. He attended Gettysburg College where he majored in Business Administration. He has been a tennis instructor, a federal bureaucrat, an ecological researcher, a teacher at a university, director of a small botanic garden, and a candidate for public office. Along the way, he took a few years off to live on a commune where he learned to milk cows and weave hammocks. Now retired, he has taken up creative writing and is drafting his first novel, *The Flora of Heaven*. He lives with his wife in a quiet village in rural upper Bucks County.

Emily Thompson

Emily is a long time reader and writer of fiction. She is published in *Goldfinch*, *Women Who Write*, *New Jersey Publication*, and in the GLVWG anthologies, 2014 until present.

Rewriting the Past

She has been many things at many different times. Writing is a release and a way to explore her world, real and imagined.

Rachel C. Thompson

Rachel is a musician, freelance writer and artist living in Ocklawaha, Florida. She formally lived and wrote for local newspapers and magazines and created political and joke cartoons in the Lehigh Valley. PA. Currently, she is focused on self-publishing sci-fi and fantasy novels. Her novels, *Soul Harvest*, *Aggie in Orbit* and *Dragon Fire* are available now in print and e-book as is her short story collection, *Stalking Kilgore Trout* wherever books are sold. Her short story 3 packs, *Heretic's 3 Pack*, *GLBT 3 Pack*, and *President's 3 Pack*, are available on Amazon only. Thompson will release another anthology, unnamed, and two more novels, *Book of Answers*, and *Aggie in Space* in 2019.

✝

Visit glvwg.org
and join the
Greater Lehigh Valley Writers Group

We would be happy to help you publish
in our next anthology!

37768067R00113

Made in the USA
Middletown, DE
04 March 2019